REAGAN AND THE WORLD

REAGAN AND THE WORLD

DAVID E. KYVIG

PRAEGER

New York
Westport, Connecticut
London

Library of Congress Cataloging-in-Publication Data

Reagan and the world / edited by David E. Kyvig.
    p. cm.
    Papers from a symposium held March 31–April 1, 1989 by the
University of Akron Dept. of History.
    Includes bibliographical references.
    ISBN 0-275-93565-5 (alk. paper)
    1. United States—Foreign relations—1981–1989—Congresses.
2. Reagan, Ronald—Congresses. I. Kyvig, David E. II. University
of Akron. Dept. of History.
E876.R3928   1990b
327.73′009′048—dc20   89-71037

A hardcover edition of *Reagan and the World*
is available from Greenwood Press
(Contributions in American History, Number 141; ISBN: 0-313-27341-3).

Library of Congress Catalog Card Number: 89-71037
ISBN: 0-275-93565-5

First published in 1990

Praeger Publishers, One Madison Avenue, New York, NY 10010
An imprint of Greenwood Publishing Group, Inc.

Printed in the United States of America

The paper used in this book complies with the
Permanent Paper Standard issued by the National
Information Standards Organization (Z39.48-1984).

10 9 8 7 6 5 4 3 2 1

Contents

Acknowledgments

This volume owes its existence to a variety of individuals and institutions. A Fulbright lectureship at the University of Tromsø in Norway in 1987–88 enhanced my sense of the importance for Americans of looking at U.S. foreign relations from the viewpoint of the country or region involved as well as from a domestic perspective. The Fulbright experience also introduced me to Geir Lundestad and started me thinking about how to entice him to visit my home university so that my colleagues and students could share my enjoyment in getting to know this extraordinarily wise and warm Norwegian. Conversations with Geir generated the idea of an early historical assessment of Reagan administration foreign relations, one that might involve Geir's friend John Gaddis and other internationally respected American scholars.

My colleagues in the University of Akron department of history supported the proposal of the Reagan and the World symposium to inaugurate what they intend as an ongoing series of scholarly symposia. A portion of an Academic Challenge Grant from the Ohio Board of Regents to strengthen the department's graduate program provided funds for the symposium. The department chairperson, Keith Bryant, Jr., and several members of the department, J. Wayne Baker, Barbara E. Clements, J. Clayton Fant, H. Roger Grant, Jane K. Leonard, Sheldon B. Liss, and Larry Simon participated in the planning and conduct of the symposium.

Other colleagues, Jerome Mushkat and James F. Richardson, along with Walter Hixson, who hadn't even joined the department at the time of the symposium and therefore should have escaped this burden, gave the manuscript a careful reading. Departmental secretary Edie Richeson with assistance from Mia O'Connor conscientiously transcribed the transcript of the symposium roundtable and prepared the final manuscript.

All of these contributions are gratefully acknowledged. The greatest appreciation, however, must be extended to the six scholars whose participation in the symposium amply fulfilled the expectations of its planners and significantly enlarged our understanding of American foreign relations during the Reagan administration. It is a privilege to be able to share their insights with a larger audience.

David E. Kyvig

1

The Foreign Relations of the Reagan Administration

DAVID E. KYVIG

Ronald Wilson Reagan, fortieth president of the United States, embodied paradox. Contradictions in his beliefs and behavior were never more evident than when he addressed himself to American foreign relations. Early in his presidency he could in all sincerity charge that the Soviet Union was "an evil empire." Then as his tenure drew to a close, he could, with an enthusiasm apparently no less sincere, embrace the Soviet premier in Moscow's Red Square. In 1983 at a time when significant numbers of Americans worried that he was shunning negotiations with the Soviet Union and might needlessly get the United States into war, the president casually tested a microphone by saying, "My fellow Americans, I'm pleased to tell you today that I've signed legislation that will outlaw the Soviet Union forever. We begin bombing in five minutes." Nevertheless, a few weeks later when Soviet action provoked him, Reagan bitterly denounced but took no action in response to the shooting down of a South Korean airliner. In his first term Reagan initiated an enormous defense build-up and forged ahead, despite much European resistance, with the installation of nuclear missiles in Europe that could reach Soviet targets within six minutes. Yet in his second term he signed an arms reduction treaty with the Soviets, which, among other things, removed such missiles from Europe.

Paradoxes regularly appeared in Ronald Reagan's other foreign undertakings as well. In 1981 as the Soviet Union seemed poised to invade Poland following the Solidarity workers' uprising, Reagan lifted the grain embargo that his predecessor had imposed on the Soviets for their invasion of Afghanistan. In 1983 after 241 U.S. marines died in a terrorist bombing, Reagan declared a continued marine presence in Beirut "vital to the security of the United States and the western world . . . [and] the stability of the entire Middle East." Within days he reversed himself and withdrew the troops. In 1985 the president declared that the American response to terrorism would be "swift and effective retribution," and later proclaimed to terrorists, "You can run, but you can't hide," while simultaneously his aides recommended political assassination in Nicaragua and secretly prepared to exchange arms for U.S. hostages in Iran. The list of apparent contradictions could be extended, but these examples should suffice to identify Ronald Reagan as a leader whom even admirers would admit was complex, and critics would describe as inconsistent or worse.

EVALUATING THE REAGAN PRESIDENCY

The task of appraising Reagan as a president and foreign policy leader involves trying to make sense of his many paradoxes. It requires as well a sober evaluation of his administration's eight years of dealings with foreign nations. Foreign perceptions of and behavior toward the United States must also be considered for they are as much a part of the country's international relations as are American attitudes and actions toward the rest of the world. Reaching a fair assessment of the foreign relations of Ronald Reagan's government is a formidable task. Yet with the final curtain having fallen on the first actor president, that very challenge now faces the historians in the audience.

Historians tend to be more cautious than most observers and analysts in making judgments about contemporary figures and affairs. Their reliance on verifiable evidence and sensitivity to complex, multifaceted explanations of causation and change make historians acutely aware of the dangers of rushing to conclusions based on a partial picture of the recent past. At the same time, their perspective on the process of societal evolution leads them to believe it better to judge contemporary events as part of a larger historical fabric rather than as isolated developments. The significance of some recent occurrence can best be seen, historians believe, by placing it in the framework of developments over a longer period of time. The understandably self-promotional hyperbole of journalism and political rhetoric may proclaim something "great," "revolutionary," or "unprecedented," which from a longer perspective may differ little from previous episodes or have few, if any, long-run consequences.

It is, nevertheless, important for historians to participate in the assessment of current events. Even if all the evidence is not yet accessible and judgments must be made largely on the basis of the public record, the historian's capacity to place recent events in a larger context can be helpful in making a judicious appraisal. The historian's first judgment will likely be revised when a fuller range of evidence and a more distant vantage point provide a better perspective, but even the first tentative consideration from the historian's viewpoint is useful in coming to terms with the immediate past.

Six distinguished historians undertook such an assessment when they gathered to evaluate the foreign relations of the Reagan administration a mere two months after the fortieth president left office. In a two-day symposium entitled "Reagan and the World: The Historians' First Assessment," a half-dozen scholars of international stature met as guests of the history department of the University of Akron on 31 March and 1 April 1989. The symposium provided an opportunity for John Lewis Gaddis of Ohio University, Akira Iriye of the University of Chicago, Susanne L. Jonas of the University of California, Santa Cruz, Philip S. Khoury of the Massachusetts Institute of Technology, Geir Lundestad of the University of Tromsø, Norway, and Robert Rotberg of Tufts University to compare the performance of the Reagan administration in various critical areas of the world. Respectively, these scholars addressed U.S. relations with the Soviet Union, East Asia, Latin America, the Middle East, Western Europe, and Africa.

Their appraisals of the Reagan era differed markedly. John Lewis Gaddis asserted that Reagan's Soviet policy was not only successful but was rationally determined and pursued from the

outset. Akira Iriye found much to admire in the Reagan administration's relations with East Asia, especially in respect to economic diplomacy. In contrast, Geir Lundestad was far less com-
plimentary of Reagan's relations with Western Europe, and the
three specialists on less-developed areas of the world offered
generally negative assessments of the Reagan record in their respective regions. Philip S. Khoury argued that the administration had further inflamed the volatile Middle East; Susanne L.
Jonas found Reagan's policies in Central America ultimately destructive of U.S. interests in the area; and Robert Rotberg concluded that the Reagan government's indifference allowed Africa's fundamental racial conflicts and economic difficulties to fester.
All six scholars helped draw an overall picture of an American
government less consistent in ideology than in regional preoc-
cupations. Whereas the Reagan foreign policy could shift without warning from an ideological to a pragmatic stance, it remained constantly attentive to certain areas of the world and
indifferent to others.

REAGAN'S VIEWPOINT

In order to appreciate fully these varied appraisals of U.S.
international relations during the eight years Ronald Reagan served
as president, it is important to recall the former California gov-
ernor's fundamental assumptions and acts in foreign affairs.
Reagan clearly articulated his beliefs during the four years between his near-miss at winning the Republican nomination in 1976
and his election as president in 1980. He constantly reiterated
several themes: The United States needed to hold its ground,
strengthen its defenses, and respond forcefully to challenges to
its authority and stature.

The Cold War in general and the Vietnam War in particular
shaped Reagan's thoughts on foreign policy. Gaining political
consciousness during the early years of the Cold War, serving
as an anti-communist FBI informant during his years as leader
of the Screen Actors Guild, and becoming a tireless (and well-
paid) spokesman for American free enterprise capitalism during
the 1950s and early 1960s, Reagan formed in his own mind a
sharp picture of U.S. virtue confronted by foreign, particularly

Soviet, threat. The Vietnam War, he believed, represented a severe setback in the struggle of democracy and capitalism against communism, a humiliating defeat that could have been avoided through more forceful military and diplomatic action. Reagan embraced the view, shared by many Americans in the 1970s, that the United States had suffered a disastrous and unnecessary decline in international stature because of its timidity and weakness. He scorned the contrary notion that the United States had arrogantly overreached itself and should become less assertive.[1]

Candidate Reagan was quite vocal about foreign policy matters. Beginning in 1977 he disparaged the treaties negotiated by Jimmy Carter and several predecessors that gave Panama control of the U.S. built and operated interoceanic canal. The Panama Canal, Reagan concluded, was a symbol of national power and prestige and, as such, ought to remain under U.S. control. Reagan also spoke frequently of the U.S. "window of vulnerability," embracing a highly controversial view that the Soviet Union possessed an intercontinental missile superiority that could, one way or another, force a U.S. surrender. He opposed the second strategic arms limitation treaty of the 1970s (SALT II) as a ratification of a "decade of neglect" of American defenses and a further widening of the "window of vulnerability." Finally, he repeatedly criticized the Carter administration's handling of the Iranian hostage taking, using the incident as a symbol of all that had gone wrong with American foreign relations. Reagan appealed to battered American pride as he insisted upon a more forceful, unyielding response to terrorism such as Iran's. During his four-year quest for the presidency, Reagan constantly advocated a foreign policy of strength and assertiveness.

Reagan's 1980 electoral victory over Democrat Jimmy Carter and independent Republican John Anderson, both of whom took exception to his views on foreign affairs, was widely perceived to reflect a desire on the part of American voters for a more forceful foreign policy. For many Americans, deep anguish over Vietnam had been followed by a sense of grievous weakness in international encounters. In 1980 Reagan was able to draw to his banner voters troubled by the Panama Canal treaties, outraged by revolutionary Iran's apparently unpunished outburst of anti-Americanism, and disturbed by U.S. inability to dissuade the

Soviet Union from invading Afghanistan. The election results of 1980 and their 1984 echo (when Jimmy Carter's vice president and surrogate Walter Mondale was the unsuccessful Democratic candidate) were widely read as public affirmations of Reagan's foreign policy views. The voters' verdicts provided the fortieth president with an unusually strong domestic position from which to pursue his international objectives.

ACTING TOUGH: FOREIGN RELATIONS IN THE FIRST TERM

When Iran released its U.S. embassy hostages on the day of Reagan's inauguration in 1981, the new president's bellicose rhetoric acquired increased stature. The incoming administration moved promptly to strengthen its image of muscular foreign policy by seeking substantial increases in defense spending at the same time that it sought significant decreases in most other areas of the federal budget. This belligerent message was reinforced in August when U.S. Navy fighter planes shot down two Libyan jets over the Gulf of Sidra. When the news slipped out that the president had not even been awakened for a report of these hostilities, opinions varied as to whether he was out of touch or regarded such militancy as unexceptional.

In contrast to this high-profile bellicosity, however, the new president took several steps that seemed at odds with his earlier campaign rhetoric. Ending the Carter-imposed embargo on grain sales to the Soviet Union showed more concern for economically hard-pressed American farmers than for unrelenting anticommunism. Secretary of State Alexander Haig argued unsuccessfully that at the very least the embargo should not be lifted without a Soviet pledge of a hands-off policy toward Poland, an argument that subsequently gained other adherents as the Soviet-backed Polish government imposed martial law against solidarity. Reagan softened a critical defense policy when he instructed the Pentagon to find a less intrusive and space-consuming system for basing the MX missile. Also, despite previous statements, the new president continued arms limitations negotiations with the Soviet Union, observed the restrictions of the 1972

Strategic Arms Limitation Treaty, and maintained diplomatic relations with the People's Republic of China.

Signs of firm anti-communism appeared far more often, however, during Reagan's first term. Little, if any, indication of a more benevolent view of the communist world came to the surface. Anti-Soviet rhetoric remained shrill. At his very first presidential press conference, for instance, Reagan declared that Soviet leaders "reserve unto themselves the right to commit any crime, to lie, to cheat."

Although talks continued with the Soviets regarding the limitation of nuclear weapons, each proposal the United States put forth during Reagan's first term was conceded to be a proposition that the Soviets could not reasonably be expected to accept. U.S. gestures toward disarmament appeared to be mere public relations posturing. The situation was complicated by NATO's 1979 decision to pursue the so-called two track option. European members of NATO agreed to receive U.S. midrange missiles in the future, provided that talks aimed at eliminating them began immediately. They took for granted that the United States would approve the SALT II treaty and that subsequently the missiles in question would be eliminated through negotiation before their scheduled mid-1983 delivery. Thus the Europeans were caught by surprise when the beleaguered Carter administration withdrew the SALT II treaty from Senate consideration. Soon Europe was faced with the impending arrival of the missiles. The Reagan administration insisted on deployment since START (Strategic Arms Reduction Treaty) talks, however fruitless, had begun. In both Britain and West Germany domestic opposition rose as the missiles began to arrive.

In the spring of 1983, Reagan offered another vivid demonstration that he was thinking more in terms of stronger defenses than an easing of international tensions. In a grim early March speech he described the Soviet Union as "an evil empire." Two weeks later, he proposed an entirely new space-based laser weapons system, which, he said, could shoot down missiles soon after launch and before they could reach their targets. This Strategic Defense Initiative, he declared, would provide a perfect safety shield against attack, close the window of vulnerability, and end the arms race. Caught completely by surprise, the

American military and diplomatic communities, not to mention most U.S. allies, had grave doubts about the feasibility of what quickly became known as the "Star Wars" defense. The Soviet Union, on the other hand, took SDI very seriously. The Soviets greatly respected American technology, feared that SDI could be used offensively as well as defensively, and realized that a new arms competition would further drain their already staggering economy. At first, however, the Soviets, faced with a serious leadership crisis, proved unable to respond. Premier Leonid Brezhnev, after several years of enfeebling illness, had died in November 1982. Neither Yuri Andropov nor Konstantin Chernenko, Brezhnev's two already elderly and ill immediate successors, survived more than fifteen months in office. Not until much younger and more energetic Soviet leadership emerged in March 1985 would there be a forceful response to the Reagan initiatives.

Ronald Reagan's foreign policy preoccupation with communism manifested itself most clearly in Central America during his first term. Persuaded that internal social, economic, and political turmoil in the region reflected a dangerous communist insurgency, Reagan was willing to invest heavily in efforts to strengthen conservative forces in El Salvador and Honduras. His greatest concern was the socialist Sandinista government of Nicaragua, which had come to power in 1979 in the course of a national revolution against the long-time right-wing dictator, Antonio Somoza. By March 1981 William Casey, the director of the Central Intelligence Agency, was planning covert operations in Nicaragua, and before year's end, Reagan had signed secret authorization for the CIA to fund a Nicaraguan rebel army, ostensibly to block arms shipments from Nicaragua to communist insurgents in El Salvador.

The Reagan administration had difficulty persuading a skeptical Congress to share its view of the Central American situation. In 1982 the Democratic-controlled House of Representatives adopted the so-called Boland Amendment to halt all funding of the Nicaraguan Contras, but then compromised with the Republican-controlled Senate to allow Contra aid to block Salvadoran arms shipments but not to overthrow the Sandinista government. In 1984 when Congress learned that the CIA had expanded its anti-Sandinista efforts to include placing mines in Nicaraguan harbors, both houses voted to revise the Boland Amendment to deny all U.S. funding of the Contras. By the end of his first term, Reagan had been unable to convince either Congress or, according to opinion polls, the American public that Central America posed any peril to the United States or its interests.

The Middle East presented problems of a very different sort. At the outset, the Reagan administration was hopeful that it could continue the U.S. peacemaking role in the region begun by Henry Kissinger in the early 1970s and continued by Jimmy Carter at Camp David in 1978. But American optimism began to unravel in mid-1982 when Israel invaded neighboring Lebanon. The United States sought to provide a buffer between the Israelis, the Syrians, and various Lebanese factions by sending marines to Beirut to escort Yasser Arafat of the Palestine Liberation Organization out of the city. Shortly thereafter, the marines once again were sent into Beirut to restore peace after hundreds of Palestinians were killed by Lebanese militiamen in the Sabra and Shatila refugee camps controlled by Israel. Lacking a clear mission, the marines nevertheless remained in Beirut during a year of futile U.S. efforts to find some basis for Israeli-Palestinian-Syrian-Lebanese peace. Their vulnerability became fully evident in October 1983 when a suicidal terrorist detonated a truck full of explosives in the midst of their barracks, killing 241 marines. The United States quickly withdrew not only the marines, but also, for the next four years, from diplomatic efforts to resolve the conflict that continued to decimate Lebanon.

Two days after the Beirut bombing, President Reagan announced that the United States had invaded the tiny eastern Caribbean island nation of Grenada in order to thwart a Marxist coup and rescue several hundred American medical students. Cuba was alleged to have supported the coup and the construction of a large airfield for military purposes. The sudden U.S. seizure of a largely unheard of country of fewer than 100,000 people, together with a press blackout of the proceedings, generated some skepticism about the purpose of the invasion. However, dramatic pictures of medical students kneeling to kiss the ground after being flown back to the United States, a sharp contrast to the grim pictures from Beirut only days before, helped produce widespread American public satisfaction with Reagan's handling of the Grenada invasion.

SHIFTING SCENES: FOREIGN RELATIONS IN THE SECOND TERM

Ronald Reagan won reelection in 1984 following a campaign in which domestic issues predominated. Nevertheless, the president and his supporters emphasized that in his first term Reagan had restored American military-diplomatic stature and firmness toward the Soviet Union. Little was said about U.S. policy toward either the Middle East or Central America. The awkward relationship between the democratic political process and foreign policy, the expression of the perceived public will and its execution may be illuminated by observing that much of Reagan's second term was spent pursuing better relations with the Soviet Union and explaining what were widely perceived as policy disasters in Iran and Nicaragua.

In part the shifts in Reagan administration foreign relations may be attributable to the unusually high rate of turnover among the president's principal foreign policy advisors. The mix of foreign affairs opinion and experience surrounding the president fluctuated constantly. Not one of the Cabinet-level appointees significantly involved in foreign relations (the secretaries of State, Defense, Treasury, and Commerce, the director of the Central Intelligence Agency, the ambassador to the United Nations, the Special Representative for Trade Negotiations, and the White House Chief of Staff) chosen at the start of Reagan's presidency remained in his or her position to the end. The critical coordinating and advisory position of national security councilor was filled over the eight-year term by no fewer than five men (Richard Allen, William Clark, Robert McFarland, John Poindexter, and Colin Powell). In lower ranking positions, there was similar turnover, not to mention disruption of supervision and direction for those who remained. Whether departures occurred because of policy or personality differences, exhaustion, incompetence, disgrace, indictment, or death, the voices to which the president listened, were, nevertheless, constantly changing.

The selection of a new Soviet leader, Mikhail Gorbachev, within weeks of the start of Ronald Reagan's second presidential term, assured that his last four years in the White House would be markedly different from the first four. Gorbachev was the vigorous, imaginative, and bold leader that the Soviet Union had lacked for more than two decades, and he soon changed the existing equation in U.S.-Soviet relations. Before the year was out, Gorbachev had taken the initiative in the dormant arms reduction talks. Meeting Reagan for the first time in Geneva, Switzerland, in November, he proposed a mutual nuclear weapons test ban involving on-site inspections, which the Soviets had long opposed. Reagan rejected this because it would have required abandoning SDI, the weapons system he had so vocally advocated as the perfect missile defense. The new Soviet leader came back quickly with an even bolder plan, which involved major concessions on European missiles, a 50-percent mutual cut in long-range offensive weapons, and a plan to rid the world of nuclear weapons altogether by the year 2000 in return for U.S. renunciation of space weapons. This January 1986 proposal, which the United States dismissed as propaganda, made obvious the Russian concern with SDI.

In September 1986 Gorbachev proposed an immediate summit meeting, and Reagan, abandoning his insistence on a predetermined agenda, accepted. Three weeks later the two met in Reykjavik, Iceland, for what has been called the "slapdash summit." Reagan and his advisors did not anticipate new Gorbachev disarmament proposals that went even beyond those of the previous January. The Americans had no alternatives to offer. The president came close to agreeing, on the spur of the moment, to a mutual and total elimination of nuclear weapons within ten years. In the end, Reagan's refusal to restrict SDI testing prevented agreement, and the Reykjavik summit came to naught. The White House quickly defended Reagan as having wisely avoided an agreement that would have eliminated the central features of U.S. defenses and left the Soviets with a significant advantage in conventional armed forces. However, critics charged that a poorly prepared, confused president had abandoned a real opportunity to end the nuclear arms race in order to pursue his technological fantasy of an effective Star Wars defense.

At the same time that Reagan's judgment at the Reykjavik summit was being hotly debated, his policies toward both Nicaragua and Iran suddenly came under intense scrutiny as well. A week before the Reykjavik meeting, Sandinista forces shot down a Contra supply plane and captured an American crew member, Eugene Hasenfus, who declared that his venture was CIA-funded. Less than a month later, reports began to spread from Tehran that the United States had been selling arms to Iran. Then on November 25 Attorney General Edwin Meese revealed the connection between these events with an announcement that the National Security Council had in fact not only arranged sales to Iran but had diverted profits to the Nicaraguan Contras. The outlines of what came to be called the Iran-Contra affair, a constitutional and foreign policy crisis of major proportions as well as a public scandal, began to emerge.

As revealed bit by bit by a presidential commission, congressional investigations, and various judicial proceedings, the Iranian arms sales had begun secretly in mid-1985 in an effort to secure release of Americans held hostage in Beirut. Within six months the president approved the idea of using the proceeds to fund the Nicaraguan Contras. Although few hostages were freed, the arms sales continued, as did the unusual funding for the Contras. More than a few Americans shared the view that this was a wonderful scheme for getting one enemy of the United States to finance a war against another, but most were troubled by the Iran-Contra revelations. Not only had the Reagan administration broken its public pledge never to negotiate with terrorists, but by obtaining so few hostage releases in return for providing a sizeable quantity of arms to the widely hated Iranians, it even appeared ineffectual in the way it conducted this questionable negotiation. The selling of government property at a profit to fund an activity that Congress had specifically ruled against raised even more troubling questions. The Reagan administration appeared to have ignored both good sense and the requirements of the Constitution in its conduct of foreign relations.

During the last two years of the Reagan presidency, the swirling Iran-Contra scandals constrained most U.S. foreign initiatives, but there were a few exceptions. In April 1986 U.S. jets shelled Tripoli, clearly aiming to kill Libyan leader Muammar

Quaddafi in retribution for various alleged Libyan terrorist acts. In 1987 the United States lashed back at Iran by offering protection to Kuwaiti oil tankers in the Persian Gulf. And the U.S. State Department resumed a more active mediating role in Arab-Israeli negotiations.

By far the most notable foreign policy initiative of the waning Reagan presidency involved the Soviet Union. Mikhail Gorbachev's determination to achieve arms reduction led to further proposals following Reykjavik. A notably less belligerent Reagan agreed to a treaty, signed in Washington in December 1987, for verifiable elimination of intermediate-range nuclear forces. This INF treaty had great symbolic value, especially in Europe, although it involved only about 4 percent of the aggregate nuclear strength of the two superpowers. In the spring of 1988, with his presidency fast drawing to a close, Reagan traveled to Moscow to affirm a new cordiality toward the Soviet Union. No further disarmament agreements were reached, but both sides seemed pleased with the image of reduced U.S.-Soviet tension, something that could hardly have been imagined in the early stages of Reagan's presidency.

THE REAGAN RECORD IN FOREIGN RELATIONS

Ronald Reagan left office with many of the paradoxes in his foreign policies still evident. Having criticized his predecessor for weakening the United States in the Panama Canal and Salt II treaties, Reagan proceeded near the end of his tenure to negotiate the first real disarmament agreement of the nuclear era. Despite long advocacy of a stronger, more effective American defense, he avoided direct acts of war except against nations incapable of belligerent response, such as Grenada and Libya. After demanding a build-up of military power, he used it sparingly and, in the case of Beirut, withdrew at the first sign of trouble. Having insisted on a stronger, more forthright posture in Central America, he dealt with that region by subterfuge and left office with the U.S. position arguably weaker than ever. And, finally, after having long preached the necessity of a more limited federal government, he departed Washington under the shadow of a scandal in which his closest associates were charged with having violated constitutional restraints and the popular will in a most reckless and excessive fashion.

How can the Reagan record in foreign affairs best be explained? The six scholars whose views are represented in this volume offered a variety of possibilities at the Akron symposium. John Gaddis suggested that there existed a more consistent purpose in Reagan's dealings with the Soviet Union than met the eye. Furthermore, Gaddis argued, careful examination of the full eight years of the historical record reveals that the president displayed skill and good judgment in pursuing his objectives. Susanne Jonas characterized Reagan's Central American performance in terms of rigidity rather than constancy. She perceived the president as an inflexible ideologue who damaged American interests by ignoring the social, cultural, economic, and political realities of Central America. Akira Iriye and Robert Rotberg found Reagan relatively indifferent to their regions. This attitude left him willing to place Asian and African matters in the hands of professional diplomats, with good effect in East Asia and, with some exceptions, poor results in Africa. Geir Lundestad and Philip Khoury attributed difficulties in U.S. relations with Europe and the Middle East to Reagan's lack of sensitivity to changing regional circumstances and balances.

Taken together, the six viewpoints suggest that in international affairs the Reagan administration must be judged on the basis of close inspection of its behavior in individual regions of the world. Performance was tightly bound to the degree of interest and ideological commitment in an area. Broad generalizations regarding Reagan's conduct of foreign relations, at least those that will stand up to careful scrutiny, do not come easily. This became particularly evident during the symposium's concluding roundtable discussion among the six scholars, the transcript of which brings this volume to a close. Searching for common patterns, the six found themselves repeatedly drawn to differences: in attitudes and ideological rigidity toward various regions, in the nature and degree of attention given each region, in the extent of autonomy accorded lower ranking regional specialists in the foreign policy bureaucracy, and finally, and perhaps most importantly, between the carefully crafted public images and the actual practices of Reagan administration foreign relations.

Ronald Reagan came to the presidency with a strong sense of the democratic, capitalist United States as an exceptional nation upon which others would be wise to model themselves. Societies striving to do so, those of Western Europe and East Asia, did not require a great deal of attention, he assumed. On the other hand, societies that rejected the American example, whether Nicaragua, Grenada, or the Soviet Union, must be dealt with firmly. And societies with different priorities, the religiously preoccupied Middle East or racially conflicted Africa, he treated with indifference, acting according to the needs of the moment or, more often, ignoring them.

Reagan's notions of how he must deal with certain situations may have changed as his experience in the presidency grew, but his fundamental perceptions did not. The apparent paradoxes of his foreign relations stemmed from the limitations and unevenness of his knowledge of the world. Furthermore, they resulted from the wide variations in vigor, insight, political skill, and influence of subordinates dealing with different regions. The paradoxes came as well from the conflicts between his ideological suppositions and his genuine desire to resolve issues. Finally, they could be explained by a widely varying degree of concern, depending on the topic and the moment, for diplomatic and constitutional procedures as well as the consequences of words or deeds.

A mixed record emerges from the appraisals that follow of the Reagan administration's relations with the rest of the world. There are indications of poor judgment and inconsistency, not to mention questions about the extent to which the president himself controlled or was even aware of specific policies and activities. On the other hand, evidence of shrewdness and achievement presents itself from time to time. Still hidden aspects of Reagan foreign relations will require a great deal more investigation before a clear picture comes into focus. Some distance from events will be helpful, too, in order to put their long-term importance, or lack thereof, into perspective. Yet for the moment at least the following essays and discussion offer a sound evaluation of the

Reagan administration's foreign relations. In the final analysis, they make clear the contribution to an understanding of the recent past that can be provided by an immediate thoughtful consideration of contemporary affairs by knowledgeable historians.

NOTE

1. To date the fullest and most useful study of the development of Ronald Reagan's ideas and career is Garry Wills, *Reagan's America: Innocents at Home* (New York: Doubleday, 1987).

2

The Reagan Administration and Soviet-American Relations

JOHN LEWIS GADDIS

The task of the historian is, very largely, one of explaining how we got from where we were to where we are today. To say that the Reagan administration's policy toward the Soviet Union is going to pose special challenges to historians is to understate the matter. Rarely has there been a greater gap between expectations held for an administration at the beginning of its term and the results it actually produced. The last thing one would have expected at the time Ronald Reagan took office in 1981 was that he would use his eight years in the White House to rebuild the domestic base of support for detente with the USSR. I am not at all sure that Reagan himself expected this result. And yet, that is what happened, with—admittedly—some help from Mikhail Gorbachev.

The question of how this happened—and to what extent it was the product of accident or of conscious design—is one that is likely to preoccupy scholars for years to come. The comments that follow are a rough first attempt to grapple with that question. Because we lack access to the archives or even to very much memoir material as yet, they are, of necessity, preliminary, incomplete, and almost certainly in several places dead wrong. Those are the hazards of working with contemporary

This essay is adapted from John Lewis Gaddis, *Russia, the Soviet Union, and the United States: An Interpretive History,* 2nd ed. (New York: McGraw-Hill, 1990), and appears here by permission.

history, though; if historians are not willing to run these risks, political scientists and journalists surely will. That prospect in itself, for a historian, provides sufficient justification for plunging ahead.

EARLY REAGAN-SOVIET RELATIONS

It is a bit difficult, now, to recall how far Soviet-American relations had deteriorated at the time Ronald Reagan entered the White House. Some of the responsibility for this rested with Jimmy Carter; at a time when defeat in Vietnam had severely shaken American self-confidence, when the energy crisis appeared to be demonstrating American impotence, when the military balance seemed to be shifting in the Russians' favor, and when the domestic consensus in favor of detente was rapidly dissolving, President Carter chose to launch an unprecedented attempt to shift the entire basis of foreign policy from that of power to that of principle.[1] His timing was terrible; his execution of policy was haphazard and inconsistent; only his intentions were praiseworthy, and in the climate of the late 1970s, praiseworthy intentions were not enough.

But the primary responsibility for the decline of detente must rest with the Soviet Union itself, and its increasingly senescent leader, Leonid Brezhnev. Given the long-term economic and social problems that confronted it, the Kremlin needed detente even more than the Americans did. And yet, Brezhnev had been unable to see that he had, in Carter, an American counterpart who sincerely shared that objective; instead he chose to view the administration's fumbling earnestness as a sinister plot directed against Soviet interests. As if to compound this error, Brezhnev also allowed Soviet foreign policy to get caught up in the same pattern of imperial overextension that had afflicted the United States in the 1950s and 1960s: just as the Americans had felt obliged, during those years, to prevent the coming to power of Third World Marxist governments, so the Russians now believed it necessary to sustain such governments, whatever the effect on the Soviet economy, on relations with Washington, or on Moscow's overall reputation in world affairs. By equating expansionism with defense, Brezhnev made the same mistake

Stalin had made in the late 1940s: he brought about what he must have most feared. It could not have been reassuring to know, as the Soviet leader approached the end of his political career, that the invasion of Afghanistan had brought about a precipitous loss of Soviet influence in the Third World; that a new American military build-up was underway with widespread domestic support; that an unusually determined NATO alliance had decided to deploy a new generation of missiles capable of striking Moscow itself; that detente was dead; and, most unsettling of all, that Ronald Reagan had become president of the United States.

To be sure, Soviet behavior was by no means the only reason for Reagan's victory in 1980. Carter and his advisers had provoked the ire of voters on a score of issues quite apart from their handling of the Russians. But these inadequacies, taken together, had conveyed an unmistakable impression of weakness and irresolution; the effect could only be to place Carter at a greater disadvantage than Gerald Ford had been four years earlier as voters assessed his record in dealing with Moscow. Reagan had come close to denying Ford the 1976 Republican nomination with charges that detente had failed to prevent Soviet expansionism. Carter's failures made him an even easier target, and Reagan quite decisively defeated him, running on a platform that called for rejection of the SALT II treaty, a rapid increase in defense spending that would produce military superiority over the Soviet Union, and a return to containment in its most militant form.

There was little visible evidence, at the time Reagan took office, that the new president expected anything other than a renewed Cold War. In his first White House press conference he asserted that the Soviet Union had used detente as "a one-way street . . . to pursue its own aims," that those included "the promotion of world revolution and a one-world Socialist or Communist state," and that "they reserve unto themselves the right to commit any crime, to lie, to cheat, in order to attain that."[2]

Key foreign policy appointments appeared to reflect this hard line. Reagan named as secretary of state the hyperbolic former general Alexander M. Haig, Jr.; contemptuous of what he would later characterize as "the Carter experiment in obsequiousness," Haig warned that the Soviet Union's "tremendous accumulation of armed might has produced perhaps the most complete reversal of global power relationships ever seen in a period of relative peace."[3] The new president entrusted the Defense Department to Caspar Weinberger, who took an equally jaundiced view of detente. Pointing out that Soviet military spending had grown "more rapidly and more steadily" during that period than in "the so-called Cold War," Weinberger quickly raised projected increases in defense expenditures that had already begun under Carter, authorized significant improvements in ground combat readiness, reinstituted the B-1 bomber program that Carter had cancelled, and approved construction of a 600-ship navy that would now have the task, if war came, not simply of protecting sea lanes but of actually attacking the Soviet navy in its own home ports.[4]

Arms control was clearly not one of the new administration's highest priorities: indeed, the president appeared to have gone out of his way to entrust that responsibility to some of its most fervent critics. Eugene V. Rostow, one of the founders of the Committee on the Present Danger, became head of the Arms Control and Disarmament Agency; Paul Nitze, another pillar of the Committee on the Present Danger and a vociferous opponent of the SALT II treaty, took on the task of negotiating reduction in intermediate-range nuclear forces (INF) in Europe, a condition the NATO allies had insisted on before agreeing to deploy American Pershing II and cruise missiles on their territory. Equally striking were the appointments of Harvard historian Richard Pipes as chief Soviet specialist on the National Security Council (Pipes headed the 1976 "Team B" exercise that had criticized the Central Intelligence Agency for underestimating Soviet strategic capabilities) and, as Assistant Secretary of Defense for International Security Policy, of Richard Perle, a long-time staff aide to Senator Henry Jackson and an ardent foe of arms control in all its forms: characteristically, Perle worried that Nitze might be too soft in dealing with the Russians and actually agree to something.[5]

The administration's proposals on arms control seemed designed to subvert rather than to advance that process. Perle him-

self proposed the elimination of *all* Soviet SS-20 missiles, whether
in Europe or Asia, in return for NATO's agreement not to deploy Pershing II and cruise missiles. Despite complaints that the
Russians would never agree to trade actual missiles for non-
existent ones (the NATO deployment was not to take place until
1983), President Reagan endorsed this "zero option" late in 1981,
thereby confirming his critics' suspicion that he was not really
interested in reaching an INF agreement.[6] At the same time,
Rostow and other advisers had recommended shifting the focus
of strategic arms talks from "limitation" to "reduction"—the
new acronym would be START instead of SALT—and in May
1982 Reagan accepted this proposal as well, calling publicly for
deep cuts in land-based ballistic missile warheads on each side.[7]
But because START would have required disproportionate cuts
on the Soviet side—seven out of every ten of their ICBMs were
land-based, as opposed to two out of ten for the United States—
most observers regarded it, along with the "zero option," as an
effort to stalemate arms control negotiations rather than as a
sincere attempt to achieve the real reductions the two proposals
professed to seek.[8]

Meanwhile, President Reagan and his advisers had quickly
gained a reputation for irresponsibility, even recklessness, on
nuclear issues. The administration's obvious preference for rearmament over arms control contributed to this; so, too, had a
series of injudicious remarks by key officials about the development of nuclear "war-fighting strategies," the firing of nuclear
"warning shots," and, in one case, the possibility of surviving a
nuclear attack provided everyone had "enough shovels" to build
backyard bomb shelters.[9] By the end of 1982 there had developed, as a consequence, the strongest upsurge in public concern
over the danger of nuclear war since the Cuban missile crisis: in
Europe this concern took the form of demonstrations against the
planned 1983 deployment of Pershing II and cruise missiles; in
the United States it produced a widespread movement calling
for an immediate "freeze" on the production, testing, and deployment of both Soviet and American nuclear weapons, a proposal popular enough to win in eight out of nine states where it
was placed on the ballot in the November elections.[10]

It was with advocates of the "freeze" very much in mind that

President Reagan in March 1983 made his most memorable pro-
nouncement on the Soviet Union: condemning the tendency of
his critics to hold both sides responsible for the nuclear arms
race, he denounced the USSR as an "evil empire" and as "the
focus of evil in the modern world." [11] Two weeks later, the president surprised even his closest associates by calling for a long-
term research and development program to create defenses against
attacks by strategic missiles, with a view, ultimately, to "rendering these nuclear weapons impotent and obsolete." [12] The
Strategic Defense Initiative was the most fundamental challenge
to existing orthodoxies on arms control since negotiations with
the Russians on that subject had begun almost three decades
earlier, and once again it called into question the president's se-
riousness in seeking an end to—or even a significant moderation
of—the strategic arms race.

Anyone who listened to the "evil empire" speech, or who
considered the implications of "Star Wars," might well have
concluded that President Reagan saw the Soviet-American relationship as an elemental confrontation between virtue and
wickedness that would allow neither negotiation nor conciliation
in any form: his tone seemed more appropriate to a medieval
crusade than to a revival of containment. Certainly there were
those within his administration who held such views, and their
influence, for a time, was considerable. But to see the president's policies solely in terms of the tone of his rhetoric, it is
now clear, would have been quite wrong.

President Reagan appears to have understood—or to have
quickly learned—the dangers of basing foreign policy solely on
ideology: he combined militancy with a surprising degree of op-
erational pragmatism and a shrewd sense of timing. To the astonishment of his own hardline supporters, what appeared to be
an enthusiastic return to the Cold War in fact turned out to be a
more solidly based approach to detente than anything the Nixon,
Ford, or Carter administrations had been able to accomplish.

SEEKING TO NEGOTIATE FROM STRENGTH

There had always been a certain ambivalence in the Reagan
administration's image of the Soviet Union. On the one hand,

dire warnings about Moscow's growing military strength suggested an almost Spenglerian gloom about the future: time, it
appeared, was on the Russians' side. But mixed with this pessimism was a strong sense of self-confidence, growing out of the
ascendancy of conservatism within the United States and an increasing enthusiasm for capitalism overseas, which assumed the
unworkability of Marxism as a form of political, social, and economic organization. "The West won't contain communism, it
will transcend communism," the president predicted in May 1981.
"It won't bother to . . . denounce it, it will dismiss it as some
bizarre chapter in human history whose last pages are even now
being written." [13] By this logic, the Soviet Union had already
reached the apex of its strength as a world power, and time in
fact was on the side of the West.

Events proved the optimism to have been more justified than
the pessimism, for over the next four years the Soviet Union
would undergo one of the most rapid erosions both of internal
self-confidence and external influence in modern history; that this
happened just as Moscow's long and costly military build-up
should have begun to pay political dividends made the situation
all the more frustrating for the Russians. It may have been luck
for President Reagan to have come into office at a peak in the
fortunes of the Soviet Union and at a trough in those of the
United States: things would almost certainly have improved regardless of who entered the White House in 1981. But it took
more than luck to recognize what was happening, and to capitalize on it to the extent that the Reagan administration did.

Indications of Soviet decline took several forms. The occupation of Afghanistan had produced only a bloody Vietnam-like
stalemate, with Soviet troops unable to suppress the rebellion,
or to protect themselves or their clients, or to withdraw. In Poland a long history of economic mismanagement had produced,
in the form of the Solidarity trade union, a rare phenomenon
within the Soviet bloc: a true workers' movement. Soviet inef-
fectiveness became apparent in the Middle East in 1982 when
the Russians were unable to provide any significant help to the
Palestinian Liberation Organization during the Israeli invasion of
Lebanon; even more embarrassingly, Israeli pilots using Ameri-
can-built fighters shot down some eighty Soviet-supplied Syrian

jets without a single loss of their own.[14] Meanwhile, the Soviet domestic economy, which Khrushchev had once predicted would overtake that of the United States, had in fact stagnated: during the early 1980s, Japan by some indices actually overtook the USSR as the world's second largest producer of goods and services, and even China, a nation with four times the population of the Soviet Union, now became an agricultural exporter at a time when Moscow still required food imports from the West to feed its own people.[15]

What all of this meant was that the Soviet Union's appeal as a model for Third World political and economic development— once formidable—had virtually disappeared; indeed as Moscow's military presence in those regions grew during the late 1970s, the Russians increasingly came to be seen, not as liberators, but as latter-day imperialists themselves.[16] The Reagan administration moved swiftly to take advantage of this situation by funneling military assistance—sometimes openly, sometimes convertly—to rebel groups (or "freedom fighters," as the president insisted on calling them) seeking to overthrow Soviet-backed regimes in Afghanistan, Angola, Ethiopia, Cambodia, and Nicaragua. In November 1983, to huge domestic acclaim but with dubious legality, Reagan even ordered the direct use of American military forces to overthrow an unpopular Marxist government on the tiny Caribbean island of Grenada. The Reagan doctrine, as this strategy became known, sought to exploit vulnerabilities the Russians had created for themselves in the Third World. With the single exception of Nicaragua—where memories of an American "imperial" legacy still persisted—this latter-day effort to "roll back" Soviet influence would, in time, produce impressive results at minimum cost and risk to the United States.[17]

Compounding the Soviet Union's external difficulties was a long vacuum in internal leadership occasioned by Brezhnev's slow enfeeblement and eventual death in November 1982, by the installation as his successor of an already-ill Yuri Andropov, who himself died in February 1984, and by the installation of his equally geriatric successor, Konstantin Chernenko. At a time when a group of strong Western leaders had emerged, including not just President Reagan but also Prime Minister Margaret Thatcher in

Great Britain, President Francois Mitterand in France, and Chancellor Helmut Kohl in West Germany, this apparent inability to entrust leadership to anyone other than party stalwarts on their deathbeds was a severe commentary on what the sclerotic Soviet system had become. "We could go no further without hitting the end," one Russian later recalled of Chernenko's brief reign. "Here was the General Secretary of the party, who is also the Chairman of the Presidium of the Supreme Soviet, the embodiment of our country, the personification of the party, and he could barely stand up." [18]

There was no disagreement within the Reagan administration about the desirability, under these circumstances, of pressing the Russians hard: the president and his advisers did not, like several of their predecessors, see containment as requiring the application of sticks and carrots in roughly equal proportion; wielders of sticks definitely predominated among them. But there were important differences over what the purpose of wielding the sticks was to be. Some advisers, like Weinberger, Perle, and Pipes, saw the situation as a historic opportunity to exhaust the Soviet system: noting that the Soviet economy was already stretched to the limit, they advocated taking advantage of American technological superiority to engage the Russians in an arms race of indefinite duration and indeterminate cost. Others, including Nitze, the Joint Chiefs of Staff, career Foreign Service officer Jack Matlock, who succeeded Pipes as chief Soviet expert at the NSC, and—most important—Haig's replacement after June 1982, the unflamboyant but steady George Shultz, endorsed the principle of "negotiation from strength": the purpose of accumulating military hardware was not to debilitate the other side, but to convince it to negotiate. [19]

The key question, of course, was that what President Reagan's position would be. Despite his rhetoric, he had been careful not to rule out talks with the Russians once the proper conditions had been met: even while complaining, in his first press conference, about the Soviet propensity to lie, cheat, and steal, he had also noted that "when we can, . . . we should start negotiations on the basis of trying to effect an actual reduction in the numbers of nuclear weapons. That would be real arms reduction." [20] But most observers—and probably many of his own advisers—assumed that when the president endorsed negotiations leading toward the "reduction," as opposed to the "limitation," of strategic arms, or the "zero option" in the INF talks, or the Strategic Defense Initiative, he was really seeking to avoid negotiations by setting minimal demands above the maximum concessions the Russians could afford to make: he was looking for a way, they believed, to gain credit for cooperativeness with both domestic and allied constituencies without actually having to give up anything.

That would turn out to be a gross misjudgment of President Reagan, who may have had cynical advisers but was not cynical himself. It would become apparent with the passage of time that when the chief executive talked about "reducing" strategic missiles, he meant precisely that: the appeal of the "zero option" was that it really would get rid of intermediate-range nuclear forces; the Strategic Defense Initiative might in fact, just as the president had said, make nuclear weapons "impotent and obsolete." A simple and straightforward man, Reagan took the principle of "negotiation from strength" literally: once one had built strength, one negotiated.

The first indications that the president might actually be interested in something other than an indefinite arms race began to appear in the spring and summer of 1983. Widespread criticism of his "evil empire" speech apparently shook him: although his view of the Soviet system itself did not change, Reagan was careful, after that point, to use more restrained language in characterizing it. (Except on one occasion in 1984, when the president, while testing what turned out to be an open microphone, jovially announced that he had outlawed Russia forever, and was about to begin bombing it.)[21] Clear evidence of the president's new moderation came with the Korean airliner incident of September 1983: despite his outrage, Reagan did not respond—as one might have expected him to—by reviving his "evil empire" rhetoric: instead he insisted that arms control negotiations would continue, and in a remarkably conciliatory television address early in 1984 he announced that the United States was "in its strongest position in years to establish a constructive and working relationship with the Soviet Union." The president concluded this address by speculating on how a typical Soviet couple—Ivan and Anya—might find that they had much in common with a typical

American couple—Jim and Sally: "They might even have decided that they were all going to get together for dinner some evening soon."[22]

It was possible to construct self-serving motives for this startling shift in tone. With a presidential campaign underway, the White House was sensitive to Democratic charges that Reagan was the only postwar president not to have met with a Soviet leader while in office. Certainly it was to the advantage of the United States in its relations with Western Europe to look as reasonable as possible in the face of Soviet intransigence. But events would show that the president's interest in an improved relationship was based on more than just electoral politics or the needs of the alliance: it was only the unfortunate tendency of Soviet leaders to die upon taking office that was depriving the American chief executive—himself a spry septuagenarian—of a partner with whom to negotiate.

By the end of September, 1984—and to the dismay of Democratic partisans who saw Republicans snatching the "peace" issues from them—a contrite Soviet Foreign Minister Andrei Gromyko had made the pilgrimage to Washington to re-establish contacts with the Reagan administration. Shortly after Reagan's landslide victory over Walter Mondale in November, the United States and the Soviet Union announced that a new set of arms control negotiations would begin early the following year, linking together discussions on START, INF, and weapons in space.[23] And in December, a hitherto obscure member of the Soviet Politburo, Mikhail Gorbachev, announced while visiting Great Britain that the USSR was prepared to seek "radical solutions" looking toward a ban on nuclear missiles altogether.[24] Three months later, Konstantin Chernenko, the last in a series of feeble and unimaginative Soviet leaders, expired, and Gorbachev—a man who was in no way feeble and unimaginative—became the general secretary of the Communist party of the Soviet Union. Nothing would ever be quite the same again.

GORBACHEV AND REAGAN

Several years after Gorbachev had come to power, George F. Kennan was asked in a television interview how so unconventional a Soviet leader could have risen to the top in a system that placed such a premium on conformity. Kennan's reply reflected the perplexity that American experts on Soviet affairs have felt in seeking to account for the Gorbachev phenomenon. He said, "I really cannot explain it."[25] It seemed most improbable that a regime so lacking in the capacity for innovation, self-evaluation, or even minimally effective public relations should suddenly produce a leader who excelled in all of these qualities. Even more remarkable was the fact that Gorbachev saw himself as a revolutionary, a breed not seen in Russia for decades, determined, as he put it, "to get out of the quagmire of conservatism, and to break the inertia of stagnation."[26]

Whatever the circumstances that led to it, the accession of Gorbachev reversed almost overnight the pattern of the preceding four years: after March 1985 it was the Soviet Union that seized the initiative in relations with the West. It did so in a way that was both reassuring and unnerving at the same time: by becoming so determinedly cooperative as to convince some supporters of containment in the United States and Western Europe—uneasy in the absence of the intransigence to which they had become accustomed—that the Russians were now seeking to defeat that strategy by depriving it, with sinister cleverness, of an object to be contained.

President Reagan, in contrast, welcomed the fresh breezes emanating from Moscow and moved quickly to establish a personal relationship with the new Soviet leader. Within four days of Gorbachev's taking power, the U.S. president was characterizing the Russians as "in a different frame of mind than they've been in the past. . . . [T]hey, I believe, are really going to try and, with us, negotiate a reduction in armaments." And within four months, the White House was announcing that Reagan would meet Gorbachev at Geneva in November for the first Soviet-American summit since 1979.[27]

The Geneva summit, like so many before it, was long on symbolism and short on substance. The two leaders appeared to get along well with one another: they behaved, as one Reagan adviser later put it, "like a couple of fellows who had run into each other at the club and discovered that they had a lot in common."[28] The president agreed to discuss deep cuts in strategic weapons systems and improved verification, but he made it clear that he was not prepared to forego development of the Strategic Defense Initiative in order to get them. His reason—which Gorbachev may not have taken seriously until this point—had to do with his determination to retain SDI as a means ultimately of rendering nuclear weapons obsolete. The president's stubbornness on this point precluded progress, at least for the moment, on what was coming to be called the "grand compromise": Paul Nitze's idea of accepting limits on SDI in return for sweeping reduction in strategic missiles.[29] But it did leave the way open for an alert Gorbachev, detecting the president's personal enthusiasm for nuclear abolition, to surprise the world in January 1986 with his own plan for accomplishing that objective: a Soviet-American agreement to rid the world of nuclear weapons altogether by the year 2000.[30]

It was easy to question Gorbachev's motives in making so radical a proposal in so public a manner with no advance warning. Certainly any discussion of even reducing—much less abolishing—nuclear arsenals would raise difficult questions with American allies, where an abhorrence of nuclear weapons continued to coexist uneasily alongside the conviction that only their presence could deter superior Soviet conventional forces. Nor was the Gorbachev proposal clear on how Russians and Americans could ever impose abolition, even if they themselves agreed to it, on other nuclear and nonnuclear powers. Still, the line between rhetoric and conviction is a thin one: the first Reagan-Gorbachev summit may not only have created a personal bond between the two leaders; it may also have sharpened a vague but growing sense in the minds of both men that, despite all the difficulties in constructing an alternative, an indefinite continuation of life under nuclear threat was not a tolerable condition for either of their countries, and that their own energies might very well be directed toward overcoming that situation.

That both Reagan and Gorbachev were thinking along these lines became clear at their second meeting, the most extraordinary Soviet-American summit of the postwar era, held on very short notice at Reykjavik, Iceland, in October 1986. The months that preceded Reykjavik had seen little tangible progress toward arms control; there had also developed, in August, an unpleasant skirmish between intelligence agencies on both sides as the

Soviet KGB, in apparent retaliation for the FBI's highly publicized arrest of a Soviet U.N. official in New York on espionage charges, set up, seized, and for nearly a month held *US News* correspondent Nicholas Daniloff on trumped-up accusations of spying.[31] It was a sobering reminder that the Soviet-American relationship existed at several different levels and that cordiality in one did not rule out the possibility of confrontation in others. The Daniloff affair also brought opportunity, though, for in the course of negotiations to settle it Gorbachev proposed a quick "preliminary" summit, to be held within two weeks, to try to break the stalemate in negotiations over intermediate-range nuclear forces in Europe, the aspect of arms control where progress at a more formal summit seemed likely. Reagan immediately agreed.[32]

But when the president and his advisers arrived at Reykjavik, they found that Gorbachev had much more grandiose proposals in mind. These included not only an endorsement of 50 percent cuts in Soviet and American strategic weapons across the board, but also agreement not to demand the inclusion of British and French nuclear weapons in these calculations—a concession that removed a major stumbling block to START—and acceptance in principle of Reagan's 1981 "zero option" for intermediate-range nuclear forces, all in return for an American commitment not to undermine SALT I's ban on strategic defenses for the next ten years. Impressed by the scope of these concessions, the American side quickly put together a compromise that would have cut ballistic missiles to zero within a decade in return for the right, after that time, to deploy strategic defenses against the bomber and cruise missile forces that would be left. Gorbachev immediately countered by proposing the abolition of *all* nuclear weapons within ten years, thus moving his original deadline from the year 2000 to 1996. President Reagan is said to have replied: *"All nuclear weapons? Well, Mikhail, that's exactly what I've been talking about all along. . . . That's always been my goal."*[33]

A series of events set in motion by a Soviet diplomat's arrest on a New York subway platform and by the reciprocal framing of an American journalist in Moscow had wound up with the two most powerful men in the world agreeing—for the moment, and to the astonishment of their aides—on the abolition of all nuclear weapons within ten years. But the moment did not last. Gorbachev went on to insist, as a condition for nuclear aboli- tion, upon a ban on the laboratory testing of SDI, which Reagan immediately interpreted as an effort to kill strategic defenses al- together. Because the ABM treaty does allow for some labora- tory testing, the differences between the two positions were not all that great. But in the hothouse atmosphere of this cold-cli- mate summit, no one explored such details, and the meeting broke up in disarray, acrimony, and mutual disappointment.[34]

It was probably just as well. The sweeping agreements con- templated at Reykjavik grew out of hasty improvisation and high- level posturing, not careful thought. They suffered from all the deficiencies of Gorbachev's unilateral proposal for nuclear abo- lition earlier in the year. They also revealed how susceptible the leaders of the United States and the Soviet Union were to each other's amplitudinous rhetoric. It was as if Reagan and Gor- bachev had been trying desperately to outbid the other in a gi- gantic but surrealistic auction, with the diaphanous prospect of a nuclear-free world somehow on the block. As an illustration of what can happen when a summit conference gets out of con- trol, Reykjavik resembled as nothing else the 1905 meeting be- tween Tsar Nicholas II and Kaiser William II in which, in a single memorable evening, they personally negotiated and signed a treaty settling long-standing Russo-German differences, only to have their horrified governments—and allies—immediately re- pudiate it. "One should never forget," one of the kaiser's advis- ers later commented, "that a discussion between two princes is propitious only when it confines itself to the weather."[35]

Negotiations on arms control continued in the year that fol- lowed Reykjavik, however, with both sides edging toward the long-awaited "grand compromise" that would defer SDI in re- turn for progress toward a START agreement. Reagan and Gor- bachev did sign an intermediate-range nuclear forces treaty in Washington in December 1987, which for the first time, provided that Russians and Americans would actually dismantle and de- stroy—literally before each other's eyes—an entire category of nuclear missiles.[36] There followed a triumphal Reagan visit to Moscow in May 1988, featuring the unusual sight of a Soviet general secretary and an American president strolling amiably through Red Square, greeting tourists and bouncing babies in front of Lenin's tomb, while their respective military aides—each carrying the codes needed to launch nuclear missiles at each other's territory—stood discreetly in the background. Gorbachev made an equally triumphal visit to New York in December 1988 to address the U.N. General Assembly: there he announced a *unilateral* Soviet cut of some 500,000 ground troops, a major step toward arms control into the realm of conventional forces.[37]

When, on the same day Gorbachev spoke in New York, a disastrous earthquake killed some 25,000 Soviet Armenians, the outpouring of aid from the United States and other Western countries was unprecedented since the days of Lend Lease. One had the erie feeling, watching anguished television reports from the rubble that had been the cities of Leninakan and Stipak—the breakdown of emergency services, the coffins stacked like logs in city parks, the mass burials—that one had glimpsed, on a small scale, something of what a nuclear war might actually be like. The images suggested just how vulnerable both superpowers remained after almost a half-century of trying to minimize vulnerabilities. They thereby reinforced what had become almost a ritual incantation pronounced by both Reagan and Gorbachev at each of their now-frequent summits: ''A nuclear war cannot be won and must never be fought.''[38]

But as the Reagan administration prepared to leave office the following month, in an elegaic mood very different from the grim militancy with which it had assumed its responsibilities eight years earlier, the actual prospect of a nuclear holocaust seemed more remote than at any point since the Soviet-American rivalry had begun. Accidents, to be sure, could always happen. Irrationality, though blessedly rare since 1945, could never be ruled out. There was reason for optimism, though, in the fact that as George Bush prepared to enter the White House early in 1989, the point at issue no longer seemed to be ''how to fight the Cold War'' at all, but rather ''is the Cold War over?''

AN EVOLVING RELATIONSHIP

The record of the Reagan years strongly suggests the need to avoid the common error of trying to predict outcomes from attributes.[39] There is no question that the president and his advisers came into office with an ideological view of the world that appeared to allow for no compromise with the Russians, but ideology has a way of evolving to accommodate reality, especially in the hands of skillful political leadership. Indeed, a good working definition of leadership might be just this—the ability to accommodate ideology to practical reality—and by that standard, the Reagan record in relations with the Soviet Union is certainly going to compare favorably with, and perhaps even surpass, that of Richard Nixon and Henry Kissinger.

Did President Reagan intend for things to come out this way? That question is, of course, more difficult to determine, given our lack of access to the archives. But a careful reading of the public record would, I think, show that the president was expressing hopes for an improvement in Soviet-American relations from the moment he entered the White House, and that he began shifting American policy in that direction as early as the summer of 1983, almost two years before Mikhail Gorbachev came to power. Gorbachev's extraordinary receptiveness to such initiatives—as distinct from the literally moribund responses of his predecessors—greatly accelerated the improvement in relations, but it would be a mistake to credit him solely with the responsibility for what happened. Ronald Reagan deserves a great deal of the credit as well.

Critics have raised the question, though, of whether President Reagan was responsible for, or even aware of, the direction administration policy was taking. This argument is, I think, both incorrect and unfair. President Reagan's opponents have been quick enough to hold him personally responsible for the failures of his administration; they should be equally prepared to acknowledge his successes. And there are points, even with the limited sources now available, where we can see the president himself had a decisive impact on the course of events. I would mention, among others: the Strategic Defense Initiative, which may have its problems as a missile shield but has certainly worked as a bargaining chip; endorsement of the "zero option" in the INF talks and real reductions in START; the rapidity with which the president entered into, and thereby legitimized, serious negotiations with Gorbachev once he came into office; and, most remarkably of all, his eagerness to contemplate alternatives to the nuclear arms race in a way no previous president has been willing to do.

Now, it may be objected that these were simple, unsophisticated, and, as people are given to saying these days, imperfectly nuanced ideas. I would not argue with that proposition. But I would also state that whereas complexity, sophistication, and nuance may be prerequisites for intellectual leadership, they are not necessarily so for political leadership, and can at times actually get in the way. President Reagan generally meant precisely what he said: when he came out in favor of negotiations from strength, or for strategic arms reductions as opposed to limitations, or even for making nuclear weapons ultimately irrelevant and obsolete, he did not do so in the "killer amendment" spirit favored by geopolitical sophisticates on the right: the president may have been conservative, but he was not cynical. The lesson here ought to be to beware of excessive convolution and subtlety in strategy, for sometimes simple-mindedness wins out, especially if it occurs in high places.

Finally, President Reagan also understood something that many geopolitical sophisticates on the left have not understood: that although toughness may or may not be a prerequisite for successful negotiations with the Russians—there are arguments for both propositions—it is absolutely essential if the American people are to lend their support, over time, for what has been negotiated. Others may have seen in the doctrine of "negotiation from strength" a way of avoiding negotiations altogether, but it now seems clear that the president saw in that approach the means of constructing a domestic political base without which agreements with the Russians would almost certainly have foundered, as indeed many of them did in the 1970s. For unless one can sustain domestic support—and one does not do that by appearing weak—then it is hardly likely that whatever one has arranged with the Russians will actually come to anything.

There is one last irony to all this: it is that it fell to Ronald Reagan to preside over the belated but decisive success of the strategy of containment that George F. Kennan first proposed more than four decades ago. For what were Gorbachev's reforms if not the long-delayed "mellowing" of Soviet society that Kennan had said would take place with the passage of time? The

Stalinist system that had required outside adversaries to justify its own existence now seemed at least to have passed from the scene; Gorbachev appears to have concluded that the Soviet Union can continue to be a great power in world affairs only through the introduction of something approximating a market economy, democratic political institutions, official accountability, and respect for the rule of law at home. And that, in turn, suggests an even more remarkable conclusion: that the very survival of the ideology Lenin had imposed on Russia in 1917 now required infiltration—perhaps even subversion—by precisely the ideology the great revolutionary had sworn to overthrow.

I have some reason to suspect that Professor Kennan is not entirely comfortable with the conclusion that Ronald Reagan has successfully completed the execution of the strategy he originated. But as Kennan the historian would be the first to acknowledge, history is full of ironies, and this one, surely, will not rank among the least of them.

NOTES

1. The best overall treatment of Carter administration foreign policy is Gaddis Smith, *Morality, Reason, and Power: American Diplomacy in the Carter Years* (New York: Hill and Wang, 1986).

2. News conference, January 29, 1981, *Public Papers of the Presidents: Ronald Reagan, 1981* (Washington, D.C.: 1982), 57.

3. Haig statement to the Senate Foreign Relations Committee, January 9, 1981, U.S. Department of State, *American Foreign Policy: Current Documents, 1981* (Washington, D.C.: GPO, 1984), 3. The comment about Carter is in Alexander M. Haig, Jr., *Caveat: Realism, Reagan, and Foreign Policy* (New York: Macmillan, 1984), 29.

4. Weinberger address, American Newspaper Publishers Association, Chicago, May 5, 1981, *American Foreign Policy, 1981*, 39. For the navy's "maritime" strategy, see Robert W. Komer, *Maritime Strategy or Coalition Defense?* (Cambridge, Mass.: Abt Books, 1984), especially 55–63.

5. See Strobe Talbott, *The Master of the Game: Paul Nitze and the Nuclear Peace* (New York: Knopf, 1988), 168; also Jerry W. Sanders, *Peddlers of Crisis: The Committee on the Present Danger and Containment* (Boston: South End Press, 1983), 281–89.

6. Strobe Talbott, *Deadly Gambits: The Reagan Administration and the Stalemate in Arms Control* (New York: Knopf, 1984), 15–18.

7. Reagan speech at Eureka College, Eureka, Ill., May 9, 1982, *Public Papers of the Presidents: Ronald Reagan, 1982* (Washington, D.C.: GPO, 1982), 585. For the origins of START, see Talbott, *Deadly Gambits,* 222–23.

8. See Stephen S. Rosenfeld, "Testing the Hard Line," *Foreign Affairs* LXI ("American and the World, 1982"), 492, 504. For warhead figures, see George E. Hudson and Joseph Kruzel, eds., *American Defense Annual: 1985–1986* (Lexington, Mass.: Lexington Books, 1985), 93. Reagan himself later admitted that he had not realized at the time of the May 1982 speech that the Russians relied primarily on land-based ICBMs. (Talbott, *Deadly Gambits,* 263.)

9. Ibid., 224–26, 287. See also Rosenfeld, "Testing the Hard Line," 504–8; and, for a catalog of such statements, Robert Scheer, *With Enough Shovels: Reagan, Bush, and Nuclear War* (New York: Random House, 1983).

10. Spencer R. Weart, *Nuclear Fear: A History of Images* (Cambridge, Mass.: Harvard University Press, 1988), 375–88; William Schneider, "Rambo and Reality: Having It Both Ways," in Kenneth A. Oye, Robert J. Lieber, and Donald Rothchild, eds., *Eagle Resurgent? The Reagan Era in American Foreign Policy* (Boston: Little, Brown, 1987), 42–44. See also Jonathan Schell, *The Fate of the Earth* (New York: Knopf, 1982), a book that contributed powerfully to fueling this concern; and the 1983 American Catholic bishop's pastoral letter, *The Challenge of Peace: God's Promise and Our Response* (Washington, D.C.: 1983), which attempted to address the moral dimensions of the issue.

11. Speech to the National Association of Evangelicals, Orlando, Fla., March 8, 1983, *Public Papers of the Presidents: Ronald Reagan, 1983* (Washington, D.C.: GPO, 1984), 363–64. For an attempt to place this speech in a broader philosophical context, see William K. Muir, Jr., "Ronald Reagan: The Primacy of Rhetoric," in Fred I. Greenstein, ed., *Leadership in the Modern Presidency* (Cambridge, Mass.: Harvard University Press, 1988), 271–78.

12. Radio-television address, March 23, 1983, *Reagan Public Papers: 1983,* 442–43.

13. Speech at Notre Dame University, May 17, 1981, *Reagan Public Papers: 1981,* 434. See also Reagan's speech to the British Parliament, London, June 8, 1982, *American Foreign Policy: 1982,* 14–20.

14. Karen Dawisha, "The U.S.S.R. in the Middle East: Superpower in Eclipse?" *Foreign Affairs,* LXI (Winter, 1982/83), 438–52. For events in Poland, see Charles Gati, "Polish Futures, Western Options," ibid.,

292–308; and Seweryn Bialer, *The Soviet Paradox: Eternal Expansion, Internal Decline* (New York: Knopf, 1986), 213–31.

15. For overviews of Soviet economic problems, see ibid., 47–50, 165; also Robert W. Campbell, "The Economy," in Robert F. Byrnes, ed., *After Brezhnev: The Sources of Soviet Conduct in the 1980s* (Bloomington: Indiana University Press, 1983), 68–124. For the growing gap between Soviet and Chinese agriculture, see Paul Kennedy, *The Rise and Fall of the Great Powers: Economic Change and Military Conflict from 1500 to 2000* (New York: Random House, 1987), 492.

16. Francis Fukuyama, "Gorbachev and the Third World," *Foreign Affairs* LXIV (Spring 1986), especially 721–31. For the efforts of Soviet analysts to come to grips with this phenomenon, see Jerry F. Hough, *The Struggle for the Third World: Soviet Debates and American Options* (Washington, D.C.: Brookings Institution, 1986).

17. For the Reagan doctrine, see Stephen S. Rosenfeld, "The Guns of July," *Foreign Affairs,* LXIV (Spring 1986), 698–714; and Alexander Dallin and Gail W. Lapidus, "Reagan and the Russians: American Policy Toward the Soviet Union," in Oye, Lieber and Rothchild, eds., *Eagle Resurgent?,* pp. 223–26. Unlike the Truman, Eisenhower, and Carter doctrines, the Reagan doctrine formalized a strategy that was already underway. The closest thing to a definitive statement of it would not come until President Reagan's 1985 State of the Union address, delivered on February 6, 1985. *Public Papers of the Presidents: Ronald Reagan, 1985* (Washington, D.C.: GPO, 1987), 135.

18. *New York Times,* January 22, 1989.

19. For a sophisticated effort to analyze differences among the president's advisers, see Dallin and Lapidus, "Reagan and the Russians," 199–202.

20. Reagan press conference, January 29, 1981, *Reagan Public Papers, 1981,* 57.

21. *New York Times,* August 13, 1984.

22. Reagan television address, January 16, 1984, *Reagan Public Papers, 1984,* 40–44.

23. For these developments, see Talbott, *Deadly Gambits,* 350–56.

24. *London Times,* December 18, 1984.

25. MacNeil-Lehrer News Hour, December 21, 1988, Public Broadcasting Network.

26. Mikhail Gorbachev, *Perestroika: New Thinking for Our Country and the World* (New York: Harper and Row, 1987), 51.

27. White House announcement, July 2, 1985, *American Foreign Policy: 1985,* 402n. For Reagan's comment, see his reply to questions

from members of the Magazine Publishing Association, March 14, 1985, *Reagan Public Papers: 1985*, 285.

28. Donald T. Regan, *For the Record: From Wall Street to Washington* (New York: Harcourt Brace Jovanovich, 1988), 351.

29. Talbott, *The Master of the Game*, 285–88.

30. Ibid., 289–90.

31. See Nicholas Daniloff, *Two Lives, One Russia* (Boston: Houghton Mifflin, 1988).

32. Regan, *For the Record*, 376–81.

33. Quoted in ibid., 390. See also Talbott, *The Master of the Game*, 315–25.

34. John Newhouse, "The Abolitionist," *New Yorker*, LXIV (January 1989), 64. See also Regan, *For the Record*, 391–96.

35. Michael Balfour, *The Kaiser and His Times* (Boston: Houghton Mifflin, 1964), 257. For postmortems on Reykjavik, see Stanley Hoffmann, "An Icelandic Saga," *New York Review of Books*, XXXIII (November 28, 1986), 15–17; and James Schlesinger, "Reykjavik and Revelations: A Turn of the Tide?" *Foreign Affairs* LXV ("American and the World, 1986"), 426–46.

36. Michael Mandelbaum, "The Reagan Administration and the Nature of Arms Control," in Joseph Kruzel, ed., *American Defense Annual: 1988–89* (Lexington, Mass.: Lexington Books, 1988), 204–8.

37. *New York Times,* December 6, 1988.

38. See McGeorge Bundy, *Danger and Survival: Choices About the Bomb in the First Fifty Years* (New York: Random House, 1988), 583.

39. See, on this point, Kenneth N. Waltz, *Theory of International Relations* (New York: Random House, 1979), 61.

3

The United States and Western Europe Under Ronald Reagan

GEIR LUNDESTAD

In the late 1940s and early 1950s, when the basic structure of the American-West European relationship was established, the Soviet threat was seen as clear and present, the United States was the strongest power the world had ever seen, Western Europe was economically weak and politically divided, and Europe was the principal arena in the Cold War. When Ronald Reagan left office, many observers argued that with Mikhail Gorbachev the Soviet threat and, with it, the Cold War were largely gone. Reagan might still be celebrating America in terms more extravagant than those used by any of his predecessors, but the air outside the White House was rife with references to America's decline. Western Europe was moving toward economic and even some form of political unity and had a material basis that rivaled that of the United States. The situation in Europe had become stable and international conflicts now generally occurred elsewhere.

Such dramatic shifts are the stuff from which old conflicts subside and new ones arise. There was much talk about a crisis in Atlantic relations. That was nothing new. All through the history of NATO, that mainstay of Atlantic cooperation, there seemed to have been one crisis or another: the rearmament of West Germany, the European Defense Community, Suez, de Gaulle, the 1973 war in the Middle East, Afghanistan.[1] Yet, NATO remained in good shape. Whereas the American-sponsored security system in Asia and the Pacific, in the form of SEATO, CENTO, and even ANZUS, had more or less collapsed, the oldest of the Cold War alliances, NATO, not only survived, but was still an important factor in Atlantic as well as in East-West relations.

Since the structure of Atlantic cooperation was set up in the first years after World War II, it is necessary to deal briefly with that period and to sketch some of the basic developments within and challenges to the Atlantic structure from the early 1950s until 1980. The main part of this essay then analyzes Ronald Reagan's response to these developments, and challenges and the European attitude to the Reagan administration. The underlying assumption here, and also my justification for spending some time on the years before Reagan, is that the roots both of cooperation and of conflict went much deeper than that rather personal level so well covered in the media and in the political debate.

THE BASIS OF THE U.S.-EUROPEAN RELATIONSHIP

The American-West European relationship was established through the Marshall Plan in 1947, NATO in 1949, the integrated NATO Command and the long-term stationing of American troops in Europe in 1950–51. The early relationship can be defined as having had three dominant characteristics.

The first was the military commitment of the United States to the defense of Western Europe. The United States had intervened in the two world wars, but NATO was its first peacetime military treaty outside the Western Hemisphere. In addition to the treaty itself, the commitment came in two closely connected parts, America's nuclear guarantee and American forces in Europe. If the Red Army were to attack Western Europe, it would run into American troops, and this would then presumably trigger an American nuclear response.

The second characteristic was the clear leadership role of the United States. The United States could rarely dictate anything outright, and it may well be argued that Washington failed to exploit, even fully to understand its tremendous leverage. Yet, the United States not only greatly influenced global economic arrangements through the Bretton Woods institutions and GATT, but also performed the very difficult task of fitting World War II enemies (West) Germany and Japan into a wider U.S.-dominated economic and military system, basically determined NATO's military strategy, promoted integration and trade liberalization inside Western Europe, and restricted trade with Eastern Europe.

The third characteristic was the pressure the Europeans exerted on the United States to play an active role in European affairs. The worry in Europe in the first postwar years was that the United States would retreat to isolationism as it had done after World War I. With the British in the lead, the Europeans pushed first for economic assistance, then for political support, and finally for military guarantees and aid from the United States. Naturally, the Europeans could not force the Americans to do anything against their will. Somewhat similar, although considerably weaker invitations had gone largely unanswered after World War I. Now, however, European eagerness for American assistance influenced both the timing and the nature of America's commitments.[2]

The American-European relationship can be said to have rested on four main premises. The joint perception of the Soviet threat was the first. The second was the unrivaled material basis of the United States. In June 1947 British Foreign Secretary Ernest Bevin stated that ". . . the U.S. was in the position today where Britain was at the end of the Napoleonic Wars."[3] Actually, the American position after World War II was in most respects considerably stronger than the British one had been after the Napoleonic wars. In 1830 both France and Russia probably had larger gross national products than Britain; in 1870 the United States and Russia probably did. In 1945 the United States produced close to half of the world's goods and services. As the world was recovering from the destruction of the war, this share was rapidly going down, but in 1950, when the reconstruction was largely over, the United States was still producing about 40–45 percent of world GNP. Whereas Britain had traditionally had the strongest navy, the United States had now taken over that role. It also had the strongest air force and, first, a monopoly on, then, a big lead in the important new currency, nuclear weapons.[4]

Europe's weakness was the third premise. Economically most of Europe, unlike the United States, had suffered great destruction. Politically the crucial roles were no longer played by the traditional powers of Europe, but by the two newcomers: the United States and the Soviet Union. The European-dominated great power system collapsed with Hitler; the continent became divided into American and Soviet spheres. In the East the Soviet Union ruled with a firm hand, from 1948 to 1953 even with an iron grip. From this European weakness sprang the Western half of the continent's invitations to Washington. With the invitations was soon to go a state of dependency, economic, political, military, and—much vaguer but not to be underestimated—psychological.

The fourth characteristic was Europe's role as the Cold War's central arena. The Cold War started with rivalry over Eastern Europe, a rivalry that rapidly spread to Germany and then to Western Europe. Europe was, despite its weakness, the big prize in the East-West conflict. Washington and Moscow both concentrated on Europe and their reaction—or better, lack of such—to major extra-European developments, such as even the civil war in China, the world's most populous country, clearly illustrated this fact.

A SHIFTING ATLANTIC BALANCE

The four premises of the original relationship were to change considerably in the following decades. The Soviet threat was tempered somewhat after Stalin's death and much more with the coming of a detente that climaxed under Nixon and Brezhnev in 1972–73. Whereas the attitudes of the United States and Western Europe toward the Soviet Union generally developed along the same lines, two differences could still be noticed. Starting with World War II, the swings of the pendulum from cooperation to Cold War and then to detente were somewhat wider, not to way wider, on the American side,[5] and as a special version of this, the attachment to the detente of the 1970s was to run much deeper and be more universally shared in Western Europe than in America.

The position of the United States was declining. In the 1970s the Soviet Union became the equal of the United States in strategic weapons. Moscow also developed some of that global power projection capability that Washington had long had. Economically the American share of world production continued to decline from 40–45 percent in 1950 to around 25 percent twenty years later. First, the United States started to run a deficit in its balance of payments, in great part a reflection of the "costs of empire." Then, in 1971, the country experienced a trade deficit for the first time since 1883.[6]

The position of Europe was also changing. In the 1970s the production of the enlarged European Community approached that of the United States. Charles de Gaulle's opposition to "the Anglo-Saxons" had earlier served to divide Europe. With the coming of German *Ostpolitik,* the entry of Britain into the EC, and the introduction of a regular system of political consultations (EPC), more unified positions were developed, first in trade matters, later also on many political questions, such as the Middle East.

While Western Europe was strengthening its position, its role in the Cold War was diminishing. The situation in Europe was being normalized on the basis of the status quo. This normalization led to large increases in trade and in cultural and human contacts across the East-West divide. West Germany in particular derived considerable benefits from this and in the course of a decade changed from being the toughest among the hardliners to becoming perhaps the strongest advocate of East-West rapprochement.

The new Cold War conflicts occurred outside of Europe. Here, unlike in Europe, American and European perspectives frequently diverged. America had criticized European colonialism and at least some of the European commitments in the Third World (Indonesia, Angola, less so Indochina and Algeria). While the Europeans were abandoning colonialism, the United States was challenging Communist advances in Korea, Vietnam, Angola, Ethiopia, and Afghanistan.

The Korean War had presented few problems, in part because

there the Soviet Union was perceived as directly behind an explicit North Korean attack, in part because most of the American build-up, in fact, went to Europe and not to Korea. Vietnam, on the other hand, was a much less clear-cut case of communist aggression and led to a draw-down of American forces and general interest in Europe. Vietnam influenced the new generation coming up in European politics in somewhat similar fashion, too, but in a totally different direction from what World War II, the Marshall Plan, and NATO had affected older generations. In Europe, Angola, Ethiopia, and to a lesser extent even Afghanistan were seen as much as "local" conflicts as East-West issues. In any case, they ought not to topple detente on the European continent. The American perspective was more global and less exclusively oriented toward Europe.[7] From this viewpoint the results of detente seemed much more questionable. A similar shift in emphasis was evident on the economic side. With the rapid rise of Japan and the Pacific area in general, in the late 1970s America's trade across the Pacific became larger than that across the Atlantic.

How, then, were these changes in premises reflected in the basic characteristics of the American-European relationship? There was no shortage of attempts to redefine the initial Atlantic bargain. Most of the key policymakers in 1947–49 had in fact accepted, in varying degree, the two-pillar concept, with the United States and Canada as one pillar and Western Europe as the other. In practice, however, NATO had come to totally overshadow its European military-political predecessor, the Western Union. Eisenhower had pressed hard for the European Defense Community, to no avail. West Germany was primarily fitted into the Atlantic structure, only secondarily into a European one, through the reformed Western European Union. Kennedy, with his usual rhetorical flair, proposed the Grand Design and Atlantic interdependence, Nixon-Kissinger a Year of Europe (1973), and Carter a "trilateral" relationship between the United States, Europe, and Japan. These attempts had one thing in common: Little or nothing came out of them; some of them may even have worsened Atlantic relations.

The basic structure remained the same. De Gaulle and the French argued that American deterrence was not credible when the United States might have to sacrifice New York for Paris. Yet, most other European leaders felt that extended deterrence was an important factor behind the "long peace" in Europe.[8] When certain American military and political circles thought up the idea of a NATO multilateral nuclear force (MLF), in the end there was little interest on the European side, with the possible exception of the Germans. The American nuclear guarantee sufficed. The small British and French nuclear forces made little difference in the larger picture. (And the British force in particular became quite dependent on American assistance.)

The withdrawal of American forces from Europe was frequently predicted. As NATO commander, then as president, Eisenhower liked to point out that the forces were in Europe on a "temporary or emergency basis." He hoped to have them out in three or four years and thought that NATO itself might be needed for only ten to twenty years.[9] In 1971 German Chancellor Willy Brandt told French President Georges Pompidou that his *Ostpolitik* "proceeded on the . . . assumption that only a part of the American forces would remain in Europe at the end of the 1970s."[10] Yet, little happened. During the Vietnam fighting, the forces came down to 291,000 compared to a high in the 1960s of 417,000, but after the war they climbed back to 320–330,000.[11] The Nixon administration was able to beat back strong congressional attempts to bring about really substantial reductions.

The United States remained the undisputed leader on the Western side. The shift in NATO strategy from massive retaliation to flexible response was largely determined by Washington, although the practical results of the new strategy were smaller than expected.[12] (Vietnam was a major reason for that.) On the global economic side the Kennedy administration took the initiative to bring about large-scale tariff reductions in a new GATT round, and on the Atlantic side the same administration was able to stop oil and gas pipeline deliveries from West Germany to the Soviet Union.[13] In certain respects the lead of the United States was enhanced. Thus the abortive 1960 summit was the last of the more traditional three- or four-power meetings. Now the most important matters would be dealt with by the two superpowers alone.

Of course, some modifications simply had to take place. American economic assistance to Europe was discontinued in the 1950s, military assistance in the 1960s. In the 1960s West Germany in particular began to place special orders in America to offset U.S. military expenditures in Europe. The U.S. share of NATO's defense expenditures fell from 74 percent in 1960 to 60 percent in 1975, but the decline could largely be explained by the Vietnam War and fluctuations in the exchange rates.)[14] Within NATO a Defense Planning Committee was created in 1963 and a Nuclear Planning Group in 1967, but these rather limited changes primarily served to strengthen the role of West Germany and the smaller allies somewhat at the expense of Britain and France, not the United States. The creation of the Eurogroup in 1968 resulted in only a marginal strengthening of the European pillar within NATO.

Only on the economic side did changes of great significance take place. The creation of the European Economic Community (EEC) in 1957–58 and its enlargement in 1973 in some respects created a European economic pillar. The American economic position was eroding and the willingness of the Europeans to follow U.S. leadership was weakening. In the mid-1970s regular seven-power Western economic summits were initiated. In part this mirrored the devolution of economic power within the Western alliance. Matters that Washington had frequently dealt with either alone or on the basis of bilateral consultations now had to be discussed in a more formal setting with the Europeans, Japanese, and Canadians. In 1979 these economic summits also began to discuss foreign policy issues.[15]

The new seven-power summits could not bring about any Western consensus. In fact, under Carter American-European relations soured further. On the military-political side America turned away from detente; Europe wanted to continue it. When Washington pressed for a wide array of sanctions after the Soviet invasion of Afghanistan, the Europeans wanted to go only part of the distance. Various aspects of burden sharing were discussed time and again. The neutron bomb issue embittered American-German relations. Jimmy Carter and Helmut Schmidt made no secret of their dislike for each other. In the Middle East American and European strategies diverged at least from the 1973 war onward, in part reflecting different economic and political needs. On the economic side disputes about exchange and interest rates, tariffs and protectionism, growth and "locomotive strategy" flourished.[16]

These issues, at least some of them, were serious enough. At a deeper level, however, it could be argued that they reflected not only the changes in the premises of the American-European relationship, but also the tension between the characteristics of the relationship, which had changed relatively little, and its premises, which had changed a great deal.

REACTING TO REAGAN

Ronald Reagan believed in America's strength and America's mission. The new president clearly did not see the United States as declining. In his first State of the Union address, he warned Congress and the nation: "Don't let anyone tell you that America's best days are behind her, that the American spirit has been vanquished." Again and again he reaffirmed his basic creed, "the undeniable truth that America remains the greatest force for peace in the world today . . . . The American dream lives—not only in the hearts and minds of our countrymen but in the hearts and minds of millions of the world's people in both free and oppressed societies. As long as that dream lives, as long as we continue to defend it, America has a future, and all mankind has reason to hope."[17]

True, in the 1970s under Nixon and Carter, the United States had suffered setbacks. Vietnam and Iran were the two most traumatic ones. "How did this all happen?" Reagan asked rhetorically. He gave the answer himself: "America had simply ceased to be a leader in the world." America had to regain "the respect of America's allies and adversaries alike."[18] Thus the United States had to stand up to the Soviet Union and resume an unambiguous leadership role vis-a-vis Western Europe. If the United States provided the leadership, the allies would follow.

The Europeans, as had the Soviets, had become frustrated with what they saw as the Carter administration's vacillation. Consultations were fine, but on difficult issues there also had to be leadership. Yet, what the new president seemed to offer—leadership without consultations—could be just as bad. The Europeans simply insisted on being listened to much more closely than in the days of clear-cut American domination. The debate about style and leadership was closely related to the question of the content of Reagan's policies. The new firmness virtually precluded a reappraisal of the American commitment to the defense of Western Europe. That helped U.S.-European relations. The nuclear guarantee would remain. In fact, the Reagan administration saw such a need to deter the Soviets that some of its most prominent members talked openly about nuclear war-fighting and about "prevailing" in a nuclear war. This kind of public nuclear strategic thinking was too much of a good thing even for European leaders who had actually preferred the old days of massive retaliation to later forms of graduated response. This kind of talk seemed unnecessary to deter the Soviets; it only served to scare the European public. On the question of American troops in Europe, the Reagan administration modernized the troops fully and strengthened reinforcement capabilities. It came out against even relatively modest pressure to bring about a stronger European conventional effort. So, on the very important point of the American commitment to Europe, not only did Washington stand firm, but it also took away much of the incentive for the Europeans to increase their conventional strength.

The Europeans had nothing against Reagan's big increases in American defense spending, but most of them were clearly unwilling to grant even the 3 percent increase that Carter had come to insist upon. American defense spending was considerably higher than European, but, the Europeans argued, there were good reasons for that. American spending had a tendency to go in peaks and valleys, whereas in Europe the increases tended to be small but steady. As a result, over-all defense spending from 1970 to 1987 actually increased more rapidly in Europe than in the United States.[19]

The crucial problem was that Washington and practically all the European capitals had a different starting point as far as detente was concerned. Secretary of defense Caspar Weinberger shocked his European counterparts when he told them that "If

the movement from cold war to detente is progress, then let me
say that we cannot afford much more progress.''[20]

The Europeans strongly favored a continuation of serious arms
control negotiations. SDI was generally seen as a potential obstacle to a START agreement, and many wondered about its
"Fortress America" implications. And this crucial new point was
again introduced by the president without any consultations at
all with the Europeans. (In fact on SDI Reagan consulted very
few members of even his own administration.)

Although European fears of an American "decoupling" from
Europe had formed an important part of the background for NA-
TO's double-track decision of December 1979, the Reagan administration's casual public attitude toward nuclear weapons and
toward arms control in general helped stimulate a rapid growth
in European peace movements, especially in the "Arch of Angst,"
Britain, West Germany, the Benelux countries, and Scandinavia. When negotiations with the Soviets broke down, deploy-
ments of cruise and Pershing missiles started in November 1983.
That could be seen as a success for Helmut Schmidt, James Callaghan, and other fathers of the double-track decision. However,
no one seemed interested in claiming paternity any more.[21] In
fact, both Schmidt and Callaghan had left the scene and new and
more radical leaders had taken over their two parties, which in
the past had been crucial in maintaining the relative NATO consensus.

The anti-communism of the Reagan doctrine also received rather
limited support in Western Europe. Only Britain appears to have
joined the United States in militarily supporting the *mujahidin* in
Afghanistan, although the rebels had the broad support of the
European public. Skepticism was evident as far as the U.S. role
in Angola, Cambodia, and particularly Nicaragua was concerned. The issue was one both of principle and pragmatism.
The Europeans generally still held that military assistance to forces
trying to overthrow a government ran counter to international
law. Reagan's policies were also seen as unlikely to succeed and
possibly even as counterproductive.[22]

In Nicaragua even the ideologically close Thatcher government pointed to the need for a "peaceful solution." Although

Margaret Thatcher was reluctant to waste American goodwill over Nicaragua and Central America, an issue where Reagan felt strongly and British interests were quite limited, she did speak up rather forcefully and in public against the invasion of Grenada, a member of the British Commonwealth, in the fall of 1983. Differences over the Middle East persisted, although Francois Mitterand narrowed differences somewhat when he abandoned the pro-Arab position France had followed since the 1967 war. One problem for the Europeans was that, whereas they might still take a considerable interest in Third World matters, in most areas they had few means of really influencing the outcome.[23]

As we have seen, disagreement between the United States and Western Europe on so-called out-of-(NATO) area affairs was nothing new. In Europe, however, agreement had been the rule, but now even that was changing. The differences between the two sides of the Atlantic in their appraisals of Soviet intentions had never been more pronounced. Their respective reactions to the imposition of martial law in Poland in December 1981 both revealed this split and added to it. Sanctions were applied against Poland, but Washington not only wanted to go further than the Europeans on this point, but also, and more important, imposed sanctions against the Soviet Union.

The Reagan administration's sanctions included the suspension of oil and gas technology sales and high technology exports in general. In fact, Washington moved into the highly controversial area of extraterritorial rights when it prohibited the export of technology manufactured both by American subsidiaries and even by licensees of American firms.

Unlike the Germans twenty years earlier, the Europeans now refused to yield to the United States. (The British had not yielded even in 1962–63, but the quantities involved then were quite small.) The planned pipeline from the Soviet Union to Western Europe mattered for European energy supplies. The effort to regulate the activities of American companies abroad and even of European companies was seen as an infringement of European sovereignty. Many felt that the American position smacked of hypocrisy, in that Reagan's anti-Soviet view did not include a continuation of the grain embargo Carter had imposed after Afghanistan. On the pipeline issue the Europeans stood firm, and, after five months of quite bitter dispute, the United States did back down.[24]

On the pipeline issue one could indeed talk about a joint European position. To a large extent that was also true about the balance between detente, arms, and arms control. Often, however, ties to Washington were still more important than internal EC bonds. Reagan's America and Thatcher's Britain were particularly close. The two leaders got along well on the personal level. They shared much of the same right-wing ideology. Reagan needed an intimate ally in Europe, whereas Thatcher could strengthen Britain's eroded position through the link to Washington. The American role during the Falklands (Malvinas) war in 1982 added considerably to the closeness of the relationship. At first the United States tried to mediate between Argentina and Britain, but when this failed, it chose Britain. American assistance was invaluable for the British defeat of the Argentinians after an expedition halfway down the globe. Although the EC countries gave political support to Britain, it was America's aid that really mattered.

A general swing to the right on both sides of the Atlantic did not stop the American-European bickering. With the exception of the Reagan-Thatcher relationship, ideology was an imperfect guide to a country's closeness to Washington. On the very troublesome INF issue, the Reagan administration received the strong support of socialist President Mitterrand in France. The German CDU-FDP government under Helmut Kohl, which had taken over when Schmidt's SPD-FDP coalition broke down in 1982, was more interested in exploring compromises. On the other hand, had the radicalized Labour party in Britain or the SPD in Germany won the elections in the two countries in 1983 and 1987, this would probably have added to the strains not only in Atlantic relations, but also inside Europe. Thus Mitterrand made it quite evident that in Germany he preferred the CDU to the post-Schmidt SPD.[25]

U.S. CHANGES, EUROPEAN RESPONSES

In 1984–85 American policy toward the Soviet Union began to change. In his first term Reagan had not met with any of the rapidly changing Soviet leaders; in his last four years he met five times with new party chief Mikhail Gorbachev. An INF treaty was signed in December 1987; progress was made on other arms control matters, including agreement in principle on a 50 percent reduction in strategic weapons; the regional crises in Afghanistan and Angola-Namibia were defused; contacts of all kinds between East and West expanded dramatically.

The change in the Cold War was to a large extent the result of concessions made by Gorbachev, apparently primarily in an attempt to turn the Soviet economy around. Yet, there was also a change on the American side, a change that had in fact started before Gorbachev speeded matters up enormously after he took over in 1985. Many factors appear to have modified the hardline policy of Reagan's first years. The United States had gone through a considerable military, political, and psychological build-up under Reagan, and the president could argue that the nation was now acting from the desired position of strength. The Democrats in Congress and a clear majority of public opinion wanted (as did Nancy Reagan) to combine "strength" and "peace" and not stress only the first as Reagan had done in his early years.[26] The European attitude was probably important, too, particularly since it coincided with such strong currents on the American side. In addition, the outcome of the pipeline dispute meant that parts of Reagan's hard line had actually collapsed. A policy that did not have the support of Western Europe would be ineffectual, punish only American companies, and could even drive that wedge into NATO that was traditionally seen as one of Moscow's primary objectives.

With the new American-Soviet "closeness," American-European relations also improved. Nevertheless, there were still problems. In periods of East-West tension the Europeans tended to see Washington as overly rigid and ideological. This was even more clearly the case under Reagan than in similar periods in the past, primarily the 1950s. Then, when Washington and Moscow began to cooperate, fears soon emerged that the superpower duo would operate at the expense of European interests. This had been de Gaulle's criticism going all the way back to the alleged division of Europe at Yalta in February 1945. Now these fears surfaced again. Such European swings, which had their parallels on certain Atlantic military and economic issues as well, at least in part reflected Europe's state of dependency on the United States. The American swings were policy swings; the European ones could be called dependency swings.

The Reykjavik summit in October 1986 was to meet the worst expectations of the Europeans. In Reykjavik virtually every European found something to be appalled by. The right and the center were shocked by Reagan's declared objective of eliminating all ballistic missiles from the face of the earth and even, ultimately, to create a world without nuclear weapons. Disagreement over SDI apparently prevented the most comprehensive disarmament agreement ever, but Reagan's insistence on SDI only served to alienate the European left. Practically all European leaders were disturbed by the "casual utopianism and indifferent preparation" of the whole exercise. The United States had suggested dramatic changes in the nuclear commitment, one of the crucial elements in the American relationship with Europe, without even consulting the Europeans. The combined efforts of George Shultz, the Joint Chiefs of Staff, and, on the European side, Margaret Thatcher and even Helmut Kohl defused the crisis, but Reykjavik remained a symbol of what could happen.[27]

The INF agreement led to the dismantling of all land-based intermediate-range missiles, which both Reagan in America and the peace movement in Europe had favored. When Gorbachev, to the surprise of many Western politicians and observers, accepted the idea, various defense experts and military men in Europe again expressed fears of America's "decoupling" from Europe. The skeptics among the leading politicians, however, had no choice but to support the INF agreement, squeezed as they were between Reagan and the peace movement.

Despite such problems, American-European relations did improve. Cooperation with Moscow was indeed preferable to confrontation. SDI was in fact used as a negotiating lever, as the Europeans wanted; the machinery of consultation worked better; on both sides there was a certain learning from mistakes. In its last years the Reagan administration was also able to make amazing progress on various regional disputes. In Afghanistan and Angola the Reagan Doctrine could be seen as meeting with success, more than the Europeans had considered likely. This, too, strengthened Washington's position.

On other Third World issues, success was more elusive and criticism from Western Europe still strong. Central America in general and Nicaragua in particular were seen as a Reagan fiasco, although European sympathies with the Sandinistas were reduced as a result of their repression. Only Britain supported the American air strike against Libya in 1986; Thatcher may well have wanted to return services rendered over the Falklands. Many Europeans, especially in the southern countries, considered Quaddafi a big nuisance rather than a threat. (In Chad, however, the French, with American support, had sent in troops against the Libyans.) The sight of an administration that made the fight against international terrorism a top priority, actually trying to trade arms to Iran for American hostages in Lebanon undermined Reagan's credibility both with the allies and the American public. The glimpses that Irangate provided of the policymaking process in Washington exceeded the worst expectations of many observers.[28]

Many Europeans thought Reagan's policies toward Nicaragua, Libya, and Iran too emotional and saw them as reflecting a certain itch to get even with rulers who had certainly offended America, but who did not really threaten its vital interests. In the Iran-Iraq war, however, Washington pressed hard for European support to protect shipping in the Persian Gulf. The United States was importing only little oil from the Middle East, whereas the Europeans were importing a great deal (and the Japanese even more). Freedom of navigation had traditionally been an important principle, especially for the British. Several Western European states therefore did agree to send in naval ships to protect shipping—and thereby at least indirectly support Iraq over Iran.

The American aloofness from the United Nations—the refusal to pay its dues in full and to accept the jurisdiction of the International Court of Justice on the Nicaraguan issue, the withdrawal from UNESCO—met with little support in Europe, again with a partial exception for Thatcher's Britain. The whole U.S. attitude to the world organization seemed to represent another of those American pendulum swings. No one had had higher hopes for the U.N.; unrealistic expectations in turn led to a serious backlash when they could not be fulfilled.

ECONOMIC FRICTION

Atlantic cooperation had flowed in great part from the joint perception of the Soviet threat. This threat alone presumably showed that America and Europe had the most basic interests in common. Strategic-political considerations took precedence over economic ones. The early American emphasis on European reconstruction and integration is best understood in this light. Washington was prepared to face increased economic competition from Europe as long as this strengthened Europe's contribution in the fight against the Soviet Union and communism.

The United States did try to integrate the European Community within a wider economic order. This could alleviate the EC's bias against goods from the outside. The various trade rounds in GATT served this purpose. Rapid economic growth and even more rapid growth in international trade greatly helped the Atlantic economic climate. Yet, in the 1960s clear signs of divergent interests emerged. The EC's common and rather protectionist agricultural policy, established in 1966, led to a fall in American exports of the goods most strongly affected (whereas others increased). The EC's many preference agreements with countries outside Europe presented difficulties for American interests. Enlargement of the EC, although desirable for political reasons, could make the implicit, and sometimes also explicit, discrimination against U.S. goods and services even more troublesome. The change in the overall international situation in the 1970s added fuel to the economic disputes. Detente softened the Cold War; the rapid growth of the postwar era slowed dramatically; the United States ran a trade deficit; the EC became stronger.

In the 1980s there were quarrels about European steel exports, again about various aspects of the EC's agricultural policies, including increased U.S.-European competition in Third World countries, just to mention those most frequently in the news.

In the early years of the Reagan administration, the economic climate was particularly cold between the United States and France. The socialist government, which until 1984 included communist representation, undertook significant nationalization and tried to speed up economic growth by pursuing an expansionist policy. It soon became evident, however, that such a policy would only undermine the French economy as long as more conservative governments gave priority to the struggle against inflation. Despite Mitterrand's efforts to move closer to Washington and somewhat more away from Moscow than Gaullism had required, the economic question served to sharpen the public's attitude toward the United States and the Reagan administration. In September 1981, 43 percent of the French were more afraid of "the United States and its monetary policy" than "the USSR and its defense policy." One year later, 45 percent of the French considered "American interest rates and the role of the dollar" as responsible for current international tension.[29] Nevertheless, the socialists had to abandon expansionism and follow more conservative fiscal and monetary policies.

Particularly the Carter but also the Reagan administration wanted export-rich and inflation-low West Germany and Japan to pursue more expansionist policies. These countries, not the United States, or France for that matter, could provide engines of growth. The Germans and the Japanese made only small concessions to this view. European criticism of American economic policies soon became stronger than the other way around. Again, this criticism could occasionally appear somewhat contradictory. Thus when the dollar was high, there was a tendency to complain that this reflected high interest rates, which in turn drew capital away from Europe and to the United States. When the dollar later began to slide, many feared that this represented an effort to undercut European competition.

The main European criticism, however, concerned the two U.S. deficits. When Reagan took over after Carter, the yearly budget deficit stood at $79 billion. Under Reagan it ranged from $128 to $221 billion and the historical total nearly tripled. The trade deficit was so great that the United States shifted from being the world's largest creditor as late as 1982 to being the largest debtor in 1986. From 1983 the United States ran rapidly increasing deficits also in its trade with Western Europe.[30]

The Europeans complained time and again about the deficits. The budget deficit drove up interest rates. The trade deficit stimulated protectionism and was really a sign of irresponsibility made possible only by the dollar's role as the world currency. No other debtor state could take up loans in its own currency and while running huge deficits still lecture Third World debtors about the importance of fiscal discipline. Similarly, the fact that several members of the EC had relatively higher government debts than the United States did not stop them from hectoring Washington.[31]

America's leadership role had rested on its economic and military strength. The early Reagan years buttressed the military position of the United States, but in the second term there was no real growth in defense spending. Reagan was also able to instill a renewed patriotism in the American people. On the economic side, the indicators were mixed indeed. After the recession of 1981–82, economic growth continued for the rest of the Reagan presidency at a higher level than in Western Europe. On a worldwide basis the United States experienced no further decline in its percentage of total production. It remained at 23 percent of world GNP.[32] But, no one could be certain what long-term effects the two deficits, which in part had fueled the economic growth, would have on the American economy.

A CHANGING AMERICAN PRESENCE

What happened to the European invitations that had been one of the characteristics of the early American-European relationship? As soon as the Americans had committed themselves economically, politically, and militarily, there was a growing tendency to complain about the strings attached to U.S. assistance. Once the benefits of the American presence were taken for granted, cries about U.S. interference became louder and more frequent, and they came not only from the minority on the far left, which all along had protested against the American role. As Michael Howard has argued, "[We] now assume that the dangers against which we once demanded reassurance only now exist in the fevered imagination of our protectors."[33]

Yet, in many areas it was evident that the Americans were

still invited to play important roles. In the strategic area, the leading European governments had not really modified their long-held view that America should be as clearly committed as possible. The pressure for "no first use" came from certain prominent Americans and from the European peace movement, not from European governments or strategists. The INF deployment decision had sprung primarily from European worries, since the Americans tended to feel that there was little or no need for a separate European nuclear balance. Whereas public opinion in many countries reacted against aspects of the American nuclear presence in particular, support for NATO as such and for the American troops in Europe remained strong.[34]

On the economic side American investments in Europe had increased very rapidly. As late as 1957 they stood at only $1.7 billion. This increased to $24 billion in 1970 and $149 billion in 1987.[35] In the 1960s fears were expressed about "the American challenge," and certain weak restrictions emerged, but the slower economic growth of the 1970s and 1980s largely made these fears go away and in fact often stimulated competition for new U.S. investment. At the same time, in these two decades European investments in America increased more rapidly than American investments in Europe. The shoe was on the other foot. There was less talk of the Americans buying Europe than foreigners taking over America. Although much of the publicity concerned the Japanese, most of this investment was in fact European.[36]

On more specific issues the skepticism about America could be considerable. In Britain there was support for the British deterrent, whereas the public was quite divided on the presence of American nuclear weapons.[37] In France that conflict had been resolved in 1966 by withdrawal from NATO's military command. The most remarkable thing about French opinion was, as we have seen, the criticism of U.S. economic policies.[38] West Germans combined very firm support for NATO and the American troop presence as such with a growing criticism both of certain aspects of the Reagan administration's foreign policy and particular aspects of the strong Allied military presence in a country about the size of Oregon.[39] Italy and several of the smaller NATO allies also combined definite support for NATO and friendly feelings for the United States in general with negative

attitudes to Reagan's early policy on detente and East-West contacts.[40] In Spain and Greece, where the United States had been
associated with the predemocratic regimes, Washington was under pressure to reduce bases and personnel. In the Greek case
the matter was postponed; in the Spanish one NATO agreed to
fund a partial relocation to Italy. In many countries there was
rising sentiment for "European defense," but little or no enthusiasm could be found for the higher defense spending that could
make a more independent force more likely.[41]

In sum, the picture varied, but there was still an interest in
maintaining and even in strengthening at least certain aspects of
the American presence. On the other hand, little remained of the
urge to involve the Americans that had characterized the establishment of the Atlantic relationship.

CHANGING TIDES IN ATLANTIC RELATIONS

Not only did the balance between the United States and Western Europe change over time, but significant developments also
took place inside each of the two geographical units. With modern means of communication, the distance across the Atlantic in
a way became shorter. Yet, at the same time it could be argued
that this distance became wider in that the respective political
centers of gravity moved away from the two coasts on each side
of the Atlantic.

The population of the United States shifted toward the South
and the West. In 1970 the Northeast and Midwest led the South
and the West by almost 10 million people; ten years later they
trailed by ten million. The South and West were generally more
conservative than the Midwest and the Northeast. In this respect they strengthened an already important underlying difference in political climate between the United States and Western
Europe. Economically and culturally the South and the West
were also less exclusively oriented toward Europe and more
toward Central and Latin America and the Pacific. The trend in
American politics was almost too perfectly captured in the 1984
election when Reagan (West) and Bush (South) defeated Mondale (Midwest) and Ferraro (Northeast).

On the European side Britain was clearly the leading power in

1945. The Attlee Labor government played a crucial role in involving the United States more closely in Europe's affairs. The bonds between the two English-speaking countries remained close. During the course of the 1950s, however, first West Germany and then France surpassed Britain in the size of their GNPs. Under de Gaulle the French tried to combine their economic rise with a claim to political leadership in Western Europe. But West Germany was soon by far the strongest power economically, and with World War II receding in the background, Willy Brandt's *Ostpolitik* expressed the country's new-found political strength. Militarily British and French nuclear weapons were in a way balanced by German conventional strength. German and particularly French relations with the United States were weaker than Britain's, historically and in terms of language, culture, and politics.

These important trends were all bound to have a bearing on Atlantic relations, but their short-term effect can easily be exaggerated. For instance, despite the rise of the Pacific, Europe remained more important for the United States in terms of strategy and investments, and the cultural and ethnic ties were considerably stronger.[42] Inside Europe, Thatcher showed how closeness to the United States could in some respects compensate for Britain's reduced economic strength vis-a-vis France and even West Germany. Probably no two American-European leaders had been as close personally and politically as Reagan and Thatcher (although in terms of what a friendship actually accomplished, the Roosevelt-Churchill relationship during World War II was far more significant).

STUMBLING TO SUCCESS

The four premises behind American-European cooperation—the Soviet threat, America's strength, Europe's weakness, and Europe being the central arena in the Cold War—had all changed rather dramatically compared to the founding years of the relationship. In most European countries Gorbachev was more popular than Reagan.[43] The strength of the United States had declined, whereas that of Europe had increased. On the financial and investment side, one could almost talk about a reversal of roles. The United States was now borrowing from Europe, not lending. Finally, in Europe the "long peace" prevailed, whereas conflicts were found in many other parts of the world.

In the 1980s after a lot of talk about "Eurosclerosis," the EC was becoming more dynamic again. New members were added: Greece (1981), and Spain and Portugal (1986). Others promised to follow. The Single Europe Act of 1987 established the 1992 goal of sweeping away all the many small barriers that still inhibited the movement of people, goods, services, and money within the Community. The act also strengthened political cooperation within the EC. On the security side, French-German cooperation expanded and the wider membership of the Western European Union and the efforts at its vitalization also added somewhat to the European pillar.

The United States had traditionally supported European integration; it still did. At the same time, however, it was becoming increasingly concerned about protecting American economic interests. Washington emphasized that "The creation of a single market that reserves Europe for the Europeans would be bad for Europe, the United States, and for the multilateral economic system."[44]

Not only did all the organizations of the American-European relationship remain, with NATO at the center, but also the early characteristics of the relationship remained, somewhat modified, though not really by much. The U.S. nuclear guarantee remained, as did the American troops—the withdrawal of which had been frequently predicted ever since Franklin Roosevelt's comment at Yalta that they would have to be back within two years. Despite America's relative decline, Reagan had tried to exert a leadership even more emphatic than what Eisenhower had done in the 1950s and Kennedy in the early 1960s. That effort had failed, but the leadership position remained. Washington was still being invited to play a substantial role in European affairs, although the invitations were more ambiguous now than in the early period.

No systematic redefinition of privileges and burdens took place. The United States still wanted to be the leader, but it also wanted to cut its expenses. It wanted "hegemony on the cheap." The Europeans wanted more influence, but were hesitant about taking on new burdens. In many small ways the relationship was being redefined on a daily basis, but the discrepancy between premises and characteristics remained so large that, at least from a logical point of view, it seemed that a more comprehensive redefinition had to take place, and sooner rather than later.

Yet, politics is only in part logic. NATO had weathered many a crisis in the past. In part it survived because of historical and bureaucratic momentum and inertia. But that was only part of the story. The Europeans still wanted insurance against Soviet surprises, and this the United States could provide. The insurance came now, as in the early days, in the form of the nuclear guarantee and U.S. troops. The merging of the growing British and French nuclear forces could possibly establish a credible European deterrent, but that remained a rather distant prospect. In fact, despite the goals of 1992, Britain was still outside the European Monetary System (EMS). When currencies could not be tied together, how could the supreme weapon of defense?

On the American side, growing financial pressure was bound to lead to new rounds of debate on burden sharing and on the size of the American military presence in Europe. Nevertheless, it remained that the troops were not only a trigger for the American nuclear deterrent; they were also the symbol of America's close relationship with Western Europe. A substantial reduction of troops could reduce expenditures; it would also be a clear sign of America's decline.

There were problems in American-European relations, serious problems. Reagan learned the hard way that there was no easy solution for these problems. The past could not be recreated, particularly a past that had never existed. In his policies toward Western Europe, Reagan ended up by "muddling through." That was what most of his predecessors had done as well. On the other hand, the founders of the postwar American-European relationship would have been amazed by the permanence of the system they had created. In this perspective, perhaps a more appropriate phrase than "muddling through" is "stumbling to success."

NOTES

1. There is really no satisfying survey of U.S.-European relations after 1945. For useful books, see Alfred Grosser, *The Western Alliance. European-American Relations Since 1945* (London: Macmillan, 1980); Lawrence S. Kaplan, *NATO and the United States* (Boston: Twayne, 1988). For a general survey of developments in Western Europe, see, for instance, D. W. Urwin, *Western Europe Since 1945. A Short Political History* (London: Longman, 1981).

2. This argument is spelled out in my "Empire by Invitation? The United States and Western Europe, 1945-1952," *Journal of Peace Research,* 1986:3, 263-77. An earlier version of the article is found in *The Society for Historians of American Foreign Relations Newsletter,* 15:3, 1-21.

3. *Foreign Relations of the United States, (FRUS),* 1947:3, Gallman to the secretary of state, June 16, 1947, 254-55.

4. Bruce Russett, "The Mysterious Case of Vanishing Hegemony; or is Mark Twain Really Dead?" *International Organization,* 39:2, 212. For a discussion of America's position in 1945-50 compared to its position in the 1980s, see my *East, West, North, South. Major Developments in International Politics 1945-1986* (Oslo: Norwegian University Press/New York: Oxford University Press 1986), 17-28. The percentages given on the U.S. GNP as part of world GNP are based on my new study in progress.

5. For this argument, see my "Uniqueness and Pendulum Swings in American Foreign Policy," *International Affairs,* 1986:3, 405-21.

6. See the references under note 4; Lundestand, *East, West, North, South,* 194-96.

7. This point is spelled out, in fact somewhat overstated in Josef Joffe, *The Limited Partnership. Europe, the United States and the Burden of Alliance* (Cambridge, Mass.: Ballinger, 1987), 12-27.

8. The phrase is from the title essay in John Lewis Gaddis, *The Long Peace: Inquiries into the History of the Cold War* (New York: Oxford University Press, 1987).

9. Stephen E. Ambrose, *Eisenhower. The President* (New York: Simon and Schuster, 1984), 143-45; Frank Ninkovich, *Germany and the United States. The Transformation of the German Question Since 1945* (Boston: Twayne, 1988), 106.

10. Willy Brandt, *Begegnungen und Einsichten: Die Jahre 1960-1975 (Meetings and Insights: The Years 1960-1975)* (Hamburg, 1976), 348.

11. Jane Stromseth, *The Origins of Flexible Response. NATO's Debate over Strategy in the 1960s* (New York: St. Martin's 1988), 89;

Zbigniew Brzezinski, *Game Plan: A Geostrategic Framework for the Conduct of the U.S.-Soviet Contest* (Boston: Atlantic Monthly Press, 1986), 207.

12. A fine account of this change is found in Stromseth, *The Origins of Flexible Response.*

13. Alan P. Dobson, "The Kennedy Administration and Economic Warfare Against Communism," *International Affairs,* 1988:4, 599–616.

14. Lundestad, *East, West, North, South,* pp. 193–94.

15. Robert D. Putnam and Nicholas Bayne, *Hanging Together. Cooperation and Conflict in the Seven-Power Summits* (Cambridge: Harvard University Press, 1987), particularly 14–20.

16. The study by Gaddis Smith on Carter's foreign policy, *Morality, Reason, and Power: American Diplomacy in the Carter Years* (New York: Hill and Wang, 1986) contains rather little discussion of the American-European relationship.

17. *The Public Papers of the Presidents of the United States, Ronald Reagan, 1982,* 79: *1983,* 271.

18. Ibid., *1983,* 265.

19. Lundestad, "Uniqueness and Pendulum Swings," pp. 408–18; Eurogroup, *Western Defense: The European Role in NATO* (Brussels, May 1988), particularly 10–11, 18–19.

20. Raymond L. Garthoff, *Detente and Confrontation. American-Soviet Relations from Nixon to Reagan* (Washington, D.C.: Brookings Institution, 1985), 1030.

21. Joffe, *The Limited Partnership,* 72.

22. Evan Luard, "Western Europe and the Reagan Doctrine," *International Affairs,* 1987:4, 563–74.

23. Michael Howard, "A European Perspective on the Reagan Years," *Foreign Affairs,* 1987/88, 66:3, 486–88; Miles Kahler, "The United States and Western Europe: The Diplomatic Consequences of Mr. Reagan" in Kenneth A. Oye, Robert J. Lieber, and Donald Rothchild, eds., *Eagle Resurgent? The Reagan Era in American Foreign Policy* (Boston: Little Brown, 1987), 318–20.

24. Garthoff, *Detente and Confrontation,* 1033–35.

25. Joffe, *The Limited Partnership,* pp. 35–38; Peter Jenkins, *Mrs. Thatcher's Revolution. The Ending of the Socialist Era* (London: J. Cape, 1987), 302–11.

26. A good account of this is William Schneider, " 'Rambo' and Reality: Having It Both Ways," in Oye, Lieber, and Rothchild, *Eagle Resurgent?* 41–72.

27. Howard, "A European Perspective," 479–82; Strobe Talbott, *The*

Master of the Game. Paul Nitze and the Nuclear Peace (New York: Knopf, 1988), 314–29.

28. Kahler, "The United States and Western Europe," pp. 319–20; Howard, "A European Perspective," pp. 483–89.

29. Renata Fritsch-Bournazel, "France: Attachment to a Nonbinding Relationship" in Gregory Flynn and Hans Rattinger, eds., *The Public and Atlantic Defense* (London: Rowen & Allenheld, 1985), pp. 91–92. For a good short survey in English of French foreign policy in these years, see Samuel F. Wells, "Mitterrand's International Policies," *Washington Quarterly,* Summer 1988, 59–75.

30. Benjamin M. Friedman, *Day of Reckoning. The Consequences of American Economic Policy under Reagan and After* (New York: Random House, 1988), 19; Martin and Susan Tolchin, *Buying Into America. How Foreign Money Is Changing the Face of the Our Nation* (New York: New York Times Books, 1988), 194; *Economic Report of the President, 1989* (Washington, D.C., 1989), 427.

31. *Economic Report of the President, 1989,* 96–98.

32. Samuel P. Huntingdon, "The U.S.-Decline or Renewal?" Foreign Affairs, 67:2, (1988/89), 81–82.

33. Michael Howard, "Reassurance and Deterrence: Western Defense in the 1980s," *Foreign Affairs,* 61:2, (1982/83), 319.

34. Flynn and Rattinger, *The Public and Atlantic Defense,* 375–76; William K. Domke, Richard C. Eichenberg, and Catherine M. Kelleher, "Consensus Lost? Domestic Politics and the 'Crisis' in NATO," *World Politics,* 34:3, 382–407.

35. Grosser, *The Western Alliance,* p. 222; *The World Almanac and Book of Facts, 1989* (New York, 1988), 132.

36. *The World Almanac, 1989,* 132.

37. Ivor Crewe, "Britain: Two and a Half Cheers for the Atlantic Alliance" in Flynn and Rattinger, *The Public and Atlantic Defense,* 35–39.

38. R. Fritsch-Bournazel, "France," in Flynn and Rattinger, *The Public and Atlantic Defense,* 69–100.

39. Hans Rattinger, "The Federal Republic of Germany: Much Ado About (Almost) Nothing," in Flynn and Rattinger, *The Public and Atlantic Defense,* 101–74, particularly 138–47; Hans Mueller and Thomas Risse-Kappen, "Origins of Estrangement: The Peace Movement and the Changed Image of America in West Germany" in *International Security,* 12:1, 52–88.

40. See, for instance, the chapters on Italy, Holland, and Norway in Flynn and Rattinger, *The Public and Atlantic Defense;* Domke, Eichenberg, and Kelleher, "Consensus Lost," *World Politics,* 382–407.

41. See, for instance, "Through a Poll, Darkly as Ever," *The Economist,* February 21, 1987, 52.

42. See, for instance, "America, Asia and Europe," *The Economist,* December 24, 1988, 29–37.

43. See, for instance, "Western Credits for Moscow Multiply," *Washington Post,* October 23, 1988, A33, 38.

44. Speech by Deputy Secretary of the Treasury Peter McPherson to the Institute for International Economics, August 4, 1988, *USIS Economics,* U.S. Embassy, Oslo, August 4, 1988, 1; see also U.S. Department of State, Bureau of Public Affairs, *Western Europe. Regional Brief,* November 1988, 1–6; Stuart Auerbach, "Europe 1992: Land of Opportunity Beckons," *Washington Post,* March 20, 1989, 1, 24.

4

The Reagan Administration and the Middle East

PHILIP S. KHOURY

Historians looking back on the Reagan era in the Middle East may be tempted to observe that it "came in like a lion and went out like a lamb." When Ronald Reagan took office in January 1981, the Middle East was literally in flames. The Soviet Union was occupying Afghanistan and a widespread Islamic-tribal resistance movement was underway. As the Islamic revolution in Iran was raging and threatening to spill over to the Arab side of the Persian Gulf, one of the most brutal wars of modern times, between Iran and Iraq, was rapidly escalating. Meanwhile, the war in Lebanon was entering a new phase as Palestinian guerrillas and Israeli troops stepped up their raids and artillery fire across the borders between Lebanon and Israel. And, over the entire Middle East region was the shadow of an increasingly dangerous American-Soviet rivalry.

By the time Reagan left the White House, however, the Middle East actually appeared to be a much calmer region. The Soviets were in their last phase of pulling out of Afghanistan. The Islamic revolutionary regime in Iran had already lost much of its force and had turned inward for a reassessment that included admitting that the war against Iraq could not be won. Lebanon no longer seemed to pose a major threat to regional stability. Even Colonel Quaddafi was uncharacteristically quiet; the American air attack on his Tripoli headquarters in April 1986 seemed to have discouraged him from taking on new ventures abroad. Only in the Israeli-occupied territories of the West Bank and Gaza did violence seem to be on the increase. Yet, partly as a consequence of the Palestinian *intifada* or "uprising," the Reagan administration had agreed to enter into a dialogue with the Palestine Liberation Organization, the most hopeful sign of a breakthrough in the Arab-Israeli impasse since the Camp David Accords of 1978. Most important of all, relations between Moscow and Washington had dramatically improved in the era of Gorbachev.

The problem with the "lion and lamb" metaphor is that by the end of the Reagan era the Middle East may have looked "lamblike," but closer scrutiny suggests that it was actually a "lounging lion." For none of the fundamental problems at the root of Middle Eastern instability, whether in Afghanistan, Iran, Lebanon, or between the Arabs and Israelis, was really any closer to resolution. Although quieter, the Middle East remained the most explosive region in the world. It did not help that the Middle East continued to receive two-thirds of the world's arms imports, that it was suffering from a severe economic recession, owing to the world oil glut of the 1980s, or that many of its regimes were unpopular.[1] Nor did it help that countervailing political ideologies were challenging several of these regimes, most visibly ideologies associated with religious fundamentalism. Fundamentalist movements may not have caused explosions on the scale of Iran, but fundamentalism itself had not subsided among the Arabs nor in Israel where Jewish religio-nationalist groups had become increasingly popular, and where 50,000 Jewish settlers in the Occupied Territories had created a major obstacle to Israeli withdrawal, at a time when these territories were aflame.[2]

Whereas it would be preposterous to blame the United States for the various crises that wracked the Middle East in the 1980s, the Reagan administration contributed considerably to inflaming several of them either by failing to develop a consistent set of policies or by refusing to take positive initiatives when the opportunities arose.

Before World War II, America's involvement with the Middle East was mainly restricted to two kinds of activity: Protestant missionary and educational work in Syria, Lebanon, and Turkey, and oil prospecting mainly in Saudi Arabia. Neither missionaries nor oilmen were particularly well placed, however, to instruct a fledgling American foreign policy establishment as it set out to fill the vacuum created by the gradual loosening of the British and French grips on the Middle East. In the aftermath of World War II, the American foreign policy establishment was obliged to take a much keener interest in the Middle East as the Cold War unfolded.[3]

American administrations—from Truman to Reagan—have aimed to accomplish three principal objectives in the Middle East. In order of importance, they have sought to contain Soviet expansion and influence; secure regular access to the region's oil, primarily to satisfy the needs of America's allies, Europe and Japan; and secure and maintain regular open markets for American goods and capital, including weapons systems and the American expertise that must accompany them.[4]

Within the framework of these three objectives, successive administrations have tried to design an overarching policy that could be systematically applied to the entire Middle East region. The problem with the design of such an overarching policy is that no single factor—neither oil nor Islam nor any one Middle Eastern state—has been sufficiently dominant to allow the United States to craft a unified policy around it.[5] For instance, although some of the states are run on oil profits and all but Israel are populated with Muslim majorities, the most influential Middle Eastern states emerged from rather distinct and separate histories. They have been shaped by their different encounters with colonialism or imperialism, different economic and strategic advantages, different approaches to the conflict between religion and secularism, and different relations with America's main rival in the region, the Soviet Union.

American foreign policymakers have generally concentrated on two subregions of the Middle East: those countries along the oil-rich Persian Gulf and those directly involved in the Arab-Israeli conflict. Although there is some overlap between these subregions and the policies designed for them, policymakers have tended to treat the two as separate problems in need of different kinds of cures or solutions.

Until the end of the 1970s, the foundation stones of American Middle East policy were two: Iran and Israel. Iran under the shah served as the police force of the Persian Gulf and as a rampart against Soviet penetration. Israel's role was perhaps less well defined, but it was viewed as an outpost of Western democracy and values and a loyal ally against hostile Arab regimes. In the 1970s two Arab states came to be increasingly important strategic actors: Saudi Arabia and Egypt. Both countries began to coordinate their regional policies with Washington. Saudi Arabia began to use its vast oil wealth to moderate radical Arab tendencies while trying to persuade Washington to be more even-handed in its dealings with the Arabs vis-a-vis Israel. Meanwhile, Anwar Sadat steered Egypt away from Moscow and toward Washington, and made peace with Israel.

U.S. strategic thinking about the Middle East for most of the 1970s was based on the Nixon Doctrine. Because of Vietnam and the American public's fear of further direct American military involvement abroad, the Nixon administration shifted the emphasis of U.S. policy by stressing that America's regional allies now had to assume primary responsibility for their own defense and, when necessary, contribute to the defense of their region.[6] But, with the Islamic revolution in Iran in 1979, quite suddenly American policy lost its equilibrium; Washington's most prized surrogate had disappeared, only to be replaced by a violently anti-American Islamic theocracy. The collapse of the Peacock Throne, shortly followed by the Soviet invasion of Afghanistan, obliged the Carter administration quickly to rehabilitate the pre-Vietnam concept of direct American responsibility for regional defense and security, in this case in the Persian Gulf. The establishment of the Rapid Deployment Force (later renamed the Central Command), with its center in the Indian Ocean, ushered in this shift in policy. When Ronald Reagan assumed the presidency, he not only embraced the Carter Doctrine, but also considerably reinforced it.

Indeed, the Reagan administration came to office already fixated on Iran and the Persian Gulf. Reagan had devoted a good portion of his 1980 election campaign to attacking Carter's failure to secure the release of the American hostages, and it is widely believed that Carter was not re-elected because of the hostage crisis. That the hostages were released on the very day that Reagan took office perhaps tells it all.

This Reagan fixation owed much to the fear that the Islamic revolution in Iran would spill over the Arab side of the Persian Gulf, destabilize the small, weak pro-Western Arab monarchies there, and disrupt oil flows to the West; even more importantly, it was inextricably tied to the Soviet occupation of Afghanistan. We must recall that Reagan came to office asserting that nearly all unrest in the Third World was being instigated by the Soviet Union, that Moscow was the source of Third World insurgencies and international terrorism.[7] In fact, Reagan's main personal contribution to shaping Middle East policy may have been to infuse his subordinates with this idea of the Soviet Union as the "evil empire." The Soviet invasion of Afghanistan in December 1979 was thought to be merely a Soviet steppingstone into the Persian Gulf—the great Russian bear rolling down toward warm water (a euphemism for oil fields) perhaps through Iran, an unstable country that was still in the midst of a revolution and thus up for grabs. That Afghanistan's uninviting geography and lack of an adequate road network made it an unlikely Soviet steppingstone to the Gulf did not seem to register at the Reagan White House.

The Reagan administration's fixation on the Persian Gulf and Afghanistan did not extend to the other major area of policy initiative in the Middle East, the Arab-Israeli conflict, where it opted for a policy of "benign neglect." This requires some explanation given that the Arab-Israeli conflict was one of the world's most volatile regional conflicts, that both sides were armed to the teeth and quite capable of going to war, and that no other regional conflict had the same potential to draw the superpowers into the fray. The following calculus appears to have been behind the administration's policy of "benign neglect" toward the Arab-Israeli conflict.[8]

First, the administration calculated that an investment in an active American peace process was not really called for because a new Arab-Israeli war was no longer as likely a prospect, especially with Egypt militarily neutralized by its 1979 peace treaty with Israel. Without Egypt, the Arabs were in no position to challenge Israel militarily.

Second, it observed that the Saudis and their oil-rich Arab neighbors had by the early 1980s become much more alarmed about their own security, owing to the war in the Persian Gulf, and no longer appeared as visibly concerned with the Palestinian issue. Furthermore, their abilities to persuade Washington to act more evenhandedly toward the Arabs had been reduced significantly after oil prices began to plummet in 1982. There may be a correlation between serious American peace initiatives on the Arab-Israeli front and the price of oil. When oil prices were high in the 1970s, Secretary of State Henry Kissinger engaged in successful shuttle diplomacy and President Jimmy Carter produced the Camp David Accords. But, for most of the Reagan years, oil prices remained low and Western reserves plentiful, thereby reducing the Arabs' economic leverage.

Third, the administration calculated that the Israeli government would not relinquish its hold on the occupied territories of the West Bank and Gaza without significant pressures from Washington. Reagan was not predisposed to apply such pressures. He and his advisers were simply much more comfortable than Carter with the ideologically conservative Israeli government headed by Prime Minister Menachem Begin. For them, Israel was more than a repository of Western cultural values and democracy; it was also fiercely distrusting of the Soviet Union and willing to confront head-on the forces of international terrorism; and combatting international terrorism was a major plank of U.S. foreign policy under Reagan.[9]

Fourth, from Ronald Reagan's personal vantage, Jimmy Carter had carried the peace process forward about as far as it could go, taking all kinds of risks and requiring all kinds of extra presidential energy, something that did not suit a nine-to-five Reagan. And peace processes generally go nowhere in the Middle East unless the president becomes directly engaged.[10]

Thus the Reagan administration felt no real compulsion to get deeply involved in a serious Arab-Israeli peace initiative. But its "benign neglect" did not extend to Israel itself. On the contrary, the disequilibrium created by the collapse of the Iranian monarchy convinced the administration to elevate Israel to the position of Washington's primary strategic asset in the Middle East. This strategic alliance not only strengthened the U.S.-Israeli relationship more than under any previous American administration, but made it virtually impossible for Washington to manage the Arab-Israeli conflict in the ways that Carter had tried. On the contrary, Israel now had a *carte blanche* to deal with the Occupied Territories and with its Arab neighbors, including Lebanon, as it saw fit. And, as the last eight years have demonstrated, that is precisely what Israel did. It tightened its grip on the West Bank and Gaza, making them much harder for Israel to relinquish, and it went to war in Lebanon without facing any real American restraints.[11] In fact, the only restraint Israel has faced in the Occupied Territories and in Lebanon has been the resistance of their local Arab inhabitants, the Palestinians and the Lebanese.

The strategic alliance meant coordinating military and intelligence policies much more closely and increasing the amount of American financial and military aid to Israel. An influential group of advisers, including the National Security Council staff, Secretary of State Alexander Haig, and U.N. Ambassador Jeane Kirkpatrick, argued that, with the loss of Iran, Israel was the only true ally left in the region, and it was a vital bulwark against Soviet-sponsored international terrorism. Articulating this same position to the attentive American public was the now influential neo-conservative wing of the media and intellectual establishment.[12] And though Congress was not of a single mind regarding international terrorism or even Soviet ambitions abroad, the Soviet occupation of Afghanistan had unified nearly all of Congress. Furthermore, there was no serious division in Congress over Israel. Under the powerful sway of the American-Israel Political Action Committee (AIPAC) and the key American Jewish organizations that support Israel, both houses of Congress were even more committed to Israel than the Reagan administration itself.[13] For most of the Reagan years, the "counterwarnings" of the group of State Department experts on the Middle East known as the "Arabists" and the small but growing Arab-American lobby fell on deaf ears.[14]

The Reagan administration's obsession with the Soviet Union as the "evil empire" somewhat distorted its view of Soviet objectives in the Middle East. Reagan advisers consistently warned that the Soviets were poised to take advantage of all the upheaval and turmoil in the region even though the Soviets had been remarkably unsuccessful in exploiting Middle Eastern instability since the late 1960s.[15] Furthermore, Moscow was rarely the main source of regional conflict and upheaval, despite administration beliefs to the contrary. Administration assessments often ignored the fact that the Soviets concentrated almost exclusively on strategic influence and security issues in the Middle East, not on oil markets. This was because administration assessments of Soviet objectives rarely took into account Soviet perceptions of the Middle East. They failed to comprehend that what the Soviets feared most was that the Middle East would be used "as a staging ground for hostile Western military build-up" against them from right across their borders. That is why they have always been much more concerned about the so-called northern tier states—Afghanistan, Iran, and Turkey—with whom they share long frontiers rather than the more distant Arab countries to the south.[16]

THE REAGAN ADMINISTRATION AND IRAN

The Reagan administration not only embraced the Carter Doctrine, but it also consolidated that doctrine by strengthening the Central Command in the Indian Ocean and by introducing the Reagan "Corollary," which stated that Saudi Arabia would not be allowed to become another Iran.[17] The Reagan Corollary explains incidentally why the administration early in its first term was willing to wage a risky (but ultimately successful) battle against Congress, which was heavily lobbied by AIPAC, over the sale of AWACS (airborne warning and command systems) and other sophisticated military equipment to Saudi Arabia.[18]

As far as the Iran-Iraq War was concerned, the Reagan administration at first struck a neutral pose; but once Iran had driven Iraqi troops from most of the Iranian territory held by Iraq and invaded Iraq in the summer and fall of 1982, Washington began to provide "low profile support" to Iraq. Trade credits were extended to Baghdad, a certain amount of intelligence was shared, and diplomatic relations were even normalized in 1985. This official pro-Iraqi tilt was favored by the Arabists of the State Department and had the strong support of the secretary of defense.[19]

While the Reagan administration officially tilted toward Iraq, however, elements in the administration pursued a very different course behind the scenes. It is important to recall that there was a camp of Reagan officials who had totally absorbed his "evil empire" metaphor and who were animated by it in nearly all their dealings. They argued that America had the wherewithal to restore American influence over Iran, despite the obvious hostility of the Khomeini regime, and that anti-Americanism would not last forever, whereas Iran's "hostility to the Soviet Union would be more permanent on account of Moscow's professed atheism and its occupation of Afghanistan." Indeed, Islamic fundamentalism in Iran could be used as a weapon against the Soviets, as it was being used by the Islamic *Mujahidin* in Afghanistan. They also argued that there was a faction in the Iranian leadership "who were as concerned as Washington about Soviet intentions in the Persian Gulf:" the so-called moderates with whom the administration could deal. Advocates of the how to "win back" Iran policy were in place from the beginning of the Reagan years and included National Security Council (NSC) advisers Richard Allen, Robert McFarlane, and John Poindexter, and Central Intelligence Agency director William Casey. These same officials supported the resumption of covert sales of weapons to the Iranian regime by Israel, a quiet policy initiated by the Carter administration during the American hostage crisis in 1980. During its first term, the Reagan administration placed an arms boycott on Iran and forcefully urged its allies to follow suit on the grounds that the Khomeini regime was actively engaged in international terrorism. But, upon the strong advice of the CIA's Casey and the NSC, "President Reagan approved Israeli sales of U.S. weaponry to Iran, with the United States resupplying Israel to make up that country's resultant munitions deficits."[20] Approval came in August 1985 and soon crystallized into a "covert policy of selling arms to Iran in return for Tehran's promised use of its influence to free American hostages held in Lebanon."[21] Moreover, the greater coordination of intelligence sharing with Israel which the policy of "strategic alliance" had fostered already had brought some Israeli operatives directly into the loop; Israeli officials believed that Israel's principal enemy was not the revolutionary Islam of Iran, but rather the radical Arab nationalism of Iraq.[22] By January 1986 the president was prepared "to authorize direct sales to Iran in exchange for Iranian influence in releasing the U.S. hostages."[23]

The approach to Iran that Reagan administration officials and their Israeli counterparts adopted had to be covert; for one thing, the Khomeini regime would never agree to deal openly with the "Great Satan," nor would Congress or the American public easily accept an open *rapprochement* with Iran, not when American hostages were still being held in Lebanon by pro-Iranian factions there, and not when it was widely thought that these same factions had blown up the American Embassy and then the Marine compound in Beirut in 1983. American officials could not go public, but they did offer their Iranian contacts more than a Bible inscribed by Ronald Reagan and a cake; they "offered" arms and "to overthrow the Iraqi government."[24]

Did it make sense for the Reagan administration to try to restore relations with revolutionary Iran when it did? Reagan advisers argued that America's long-run interests necessitated an improvement in relations with Iran, because it was the largest regional power in the Persian Gulf and shared a 1,000 mile border with the Soviet Union. The problem was that the Iranians had their cake and got to eat it, too. The Iranian regime understood that if it played hardball with Washington it could extract otherwise unattainable concessions, as it had during the American hostage crisis in 1980, when Iran began to receive American spare parts via Israel.[25] Five years later, the Reagan administration made similar concessions, in spite of the president's "Ramboesque" rhetoric. Iran once again received arms, yet the American hostages remained captive in Lebanon. There seems little doubt that had the arms sales not become public knowledge, American officials would have continued their covert dealings with the Iranians; it seems quite unlikely that this would have restored American influence in Iran.

As a result of revelations in the fall of 1986 that the Reagan administration was secretly selling arms to Iran, U.S. policy lunged back in the other direction. Suddenly, the administration was forced to prove to its outraged moderate Arab allies in the Persian Gulf and to domestic U.S. critics that American policy was not being held hostage by Iran. Further revelations that at least one administration official, Lieutenant Colonel Oliver North of the NSC staff, "had arranged for the transference to Contra groups, via concealed Swiss bank accounts, of profits made from the Iran arms sales,"[26] only exacerbated the situation in Washington. So, what did the administration do? It accepted an invitation to protect Kuwait's oil tankers in the Persian Gulf by reflagging them with the "Stars and Stripes." Typically, the administration justified its decision with the argument that if it did not reflag Kuwaiti tankers, this would leave wide open the door for Soviet penetration of the Gulf, especially since Kuwait had also invited the Soviets to reflag its tankers. In fact, when Kuwait extended its invitation to the two superpowers at the end of 1986, the Soviets were clearly not pressing to achieve a stronger position in the Gulf. On the contrary, they were bogged down in Afghanistan—their Vietnam—and were actually trying to reduce their costly involvements in the Middle East. Moreover, the high risks the administration had now assumed in the Gulf were unnecessary because the tanker war was not particularly threatening or disruptive to the international oil market. Simply, Washington's claim that it was ensuring the free flow of oil to America's Western allies was bogus.[27] Furthermore, the main culprit in the rocket attacks on Persian Gulf shipping was not Iran in any case, but Iraq, whom the Reagan administration was supporting and whose missile struck the U.S.S. *Stark* in May 1987, killing thirty-seven American sailors.

The Iran-Contra affair revealed that the Reagan administration had no clear or consistent policy in the Persian Gulf. In the course of six years, it had gone from a policy of "ignoring Iran to secretly wooing Iran to directly confronting Iran."[28] What saved it from impending disaster—that is, the loss of large numbers of American men in uniform—was Iran's unexpected decision to give up the war in 1988. Although Ayatollah Khomeini declared that the enlarged presence of the United States in the Persian Gulf had been instrumental in the decision, domestic factors seem to have been principally responsible; the revolutionary flame in

Tehran had begun to flicker and the Iranian leadership had lost confidence that its forces could break the military stalemate of the previous two years.

That President Reagan personally managed to survive the Iran-Contra affair is quite remarkable. Although his administration suffered a severe loss of credibility at home and overseas, he miraculously escaped the worst consequences of his government's actions. It is perhaps less remarkable that American interests in the Persian Gulf also survived owing to Iran's withdrawal from the war with Iraq. The downside to Reagan's Gulf policy was increased skepticism in moderate Arab circles about America's reliability.[29]

THE REAGAN ADMINISTRATION AND LEBANON

Lebanon was where the Reagan administration became most deeply involved in its first term. Since 1975 Lebanon had been locked in a degenerating war pitting Muslims against Christians and poor against rich. But the war was not simply one of Lebanese against Lebanese; there was also a large Palestinian armed presence in the country, not to mention many other foreign influences owing to Lebanon's historically weak state structure and army. Syria, Israel, Libya, and Iran were all major players there.[30]

The Reagan administration was reluctant to become deeply involved in Lebanon. It took its cue from the Carter administration, which had virtually ignored the country because of its preoccupation with the Egyptian-Israeli peace and events in Iran. But, also, the war had significantly reduced Lebanon's importance as the leading commercial and communications center in the Arab world.[31] The security situation on the borders with Israel, however, soon encouraged the Reagan administration to broker a cease-fire between Israel and the Palestine Liberation Organization in early 1981 that lasted more than a year. The cease-fire did not prevent the PLO from operating inside Lebanon, however, nor did it stop Israel from increasing its own involvement through the cultivation of the right-wing Christian militias in Lebanon.[32]

Once General Ariel Sharon became defense minister in Begin's cabinet in 1981, much more ambitious Israeli plans for

Lebanon were prepared. The Begin government wanted to destroy the infrastructure of the PLO in Lebanon and bring Israel's Lebanese allies, the Phalangists, to power. Israel also hoped to dislodge the large Syrian military presence in Lebanon, for Syria had not only become Israel's main Arab nemesis after the Egyptian-Israeli treaty removed Egypt from the military equation, but it was also Moscow's main client in the region.[33] Ultimately, the Israeli government hoped to prop up a pro-Israeli Lebanese government, which would then sign a separate peace with Israel the way Egypt had, thereby increasing Syria's isolation. To engineer all of this, the Israeli Defense Forces were ordered to invade Lebanon in early June 1982.[34]

Although the Israeli invasion did not exactly surprise the Reagan administration, it did not seem pleased that the Israelis carried the invasion as far as Beirut. The extent to which leading members of the administration condoned the Israeli army's deep penetration may be linked to the role of then Secretary of State Haig, an admirer of Sharon and an architect of the strategic alliance with Israel; some Israeli and American experts have asserted that Haig gave Israel the "green light" for the invasion. The White House claimed that it had understood that Israeli forces would only move 40 kilometers (25 miles) into Lebanon to secure their northern border and thus ensure "Peace for Galilee," but that the Israelis had never indicated that they would drive all the way to Beirut. The invasion left 15,000 Lebanese and Palestinians dead; 600 Israeli troops were killed in the same period.[35] In any case, Haig lost his job shortly thereafter: He had already alienated a number of White House officials over other issues, and now had lost the confidence of the president.[36]

There is some question as to whether credit for deploying American marines, ending the Israeli siege of Beirut, the evacuation of the PLO with its chairman Yasser Arafat from the Lebanese capital, and the election of the Phalangist militia leader Bashir Gemayel to the Lebanese presidency should be given to George Shultz, Haig's successor at the State Department. Shultz came to his post with a reputation for being sympathetic to the moderate Arab position, owing in large part to his close association with the Bechtel Corporation, a major American engineering firm with huge contracts in the Arab world, and he may have felt the need to strike a more evenhanded pose as a corrective to Haig's strong pro-Israeli stance.[37]

What is certain is that Shultz took advantage of the somewhat improved situation in Lebanon to convince a reluctant Ronald Reagan to become involved in wider diplomatic efforts in the region by announcing on September 1, 1982 a plan for the resolution of the Arab-Israeli conflict. Rejecting Israeli annexation of the Occupied Territories as well as the idea of an independent Palestinian state, the Reagan plan called for an association of the West Bank, Gaza, and Jordan.

The plan met with a mixed reception—negative from Israel, less so from the Arabs who responded almost immediately with their own plan based on an Arab League summit meeting held at Fez, Morocco.[38] Commitment to the Reagan plan, however, "was predicated on the belief that the problems of Lebanon were on their way to a solution."[39] This was not so. The assassination of President-elect Gemayel just two weeks after the plan was announced, and, in reprisal, the systematic murder of hundreds of Palestinians in the refugee camps of Sabra and Shatila by members of Gemayel's Phalangist militia who had been invited into West Beirut by the Israeli security forces that had occupied this zone, effectively buried the Reagan peace initiative.[40]

The American response was to put Lebanon back on the agenda but to the exclusion of any activity on the Arab-Israeli peace front, something that both the Israeli and Syrian governments welcomed. Under the Camp David formula Begin had returned Sinai to Egypt, but he was unwilling to consider giving up Israeli control of the West Bank and Gaza. From Syrian President Hafiz al-Asad's vantage, Camp David had broken apart both the Arab military and diplomatic front leaving Syria increasingly vulnerable in the face of the more powerful Israeli Defense Forces.

The rest of the story in Lebanon is a sad and most humiliating one for the Reagan administration. American policy had two related aims: to rebuild the Lebanese military so that the Lebanese government could regain control of the country, and to get the Lebanese government and Israel to forge an accord that would lead to an Israeli withdrawal from the country, and, it was assumed, a Syrian withdrawal as well. The major problem with the agreement, which was actually signed on May 17, 1983, was that it offered the Syrians absolutely nothing, even though Syria had vast influence in Lebanon, including 40,000 troops stationed there. Apart from the fact that the accord ignored and completely by-passed the Syrian regime, it allowed for a continued Israeli mil-itary presence in the country until the Syrians also withdrew. President Asad believed that Washington had left the door wide open for Israel to draw Lebanon into its orbit. By his calcula-tion, Israel would continue to arm and train the Phalange militia with its considerable influence over Lebanese President Amin Gemayel, the older brother of the late Bashir; the militia pre-dictably would have greater influence over the Lebanese army; and together the army and Israel would be aligned against Syria.[41] With Egypt neutralized by its peace treaty with Israel, Iraq bogged down in its war with Iran, and Syrian-Jordanian relations at a low ebb, Syria now faced Israel all alone, not only across its own borders but also in the heart of Lebanon. Asad could not afford to allow Lebanon to move in Israel's direction if he planned to stand up and be counted in the future.

The Reagan administration's seemingly blind commitment to an accord that completely ignored one of the two main regional powers in Lebanon stemmed from two misconceptions: the first was based on the administration's firm ideological belief that Syria was a key component of the Soviet Union's "evil empire," thereby making it virtually impossible for Washington to accept that the Asad regime might have legitimate security interests in Lebanon; the second was its remarkably successful diplomacy in getting the PLO out of Beirut in the summer of 1982, which created a sense of confidence that had no grounding in reality. Administration officials in the field were convinced that the American role in Lebanon would lead to the rapid withdrawal of all foreign forces, including the Syrians who were thought to be shell-shocked and weak after their humiliating defeat at the hands of Israel. This excessive optimism rubbed off on George Shultz who accelerated the diplomatic process after receiving signals that made him think that Syria would withdraw, even though Washington had offered Asad little in return. Instead, Asad was resolved to prevent that diplomatic process from completing its course.[42]

By the spring of 1983, Asad was in a much stronger military position than he had been in June 1982 when Israel humiliated the Syrian air force in four days by destroying more than eighty fighter planes and knocking out its air defense system. Within six months, the Soviets had embarked on the largest reequipment effort in their history; the Syrian air force was renewed and upgraded, and advanced Soviet missile systems were deployed in the country, manned in part by Soviet advisers.[43] Syria was now prepared to confront the United States in Lebanon. A Lebanese Shi'ite faction in the Syrian-controlled zone of West Beirut blew up the American Embassy in April 1983, and then in October a truck bomb was detonated in the marine compound, killing 241 American servicemen. Later two American planes were shot down by Syria. The president of Lebanon, under great pressure from the Asad regime and its Lebanese clients, backed out of the Lebanese-Israeli agreement. The Reagan administration had been stung. Fears that the extensive American losses and the humiliation of being outmaneuvered by Damascus might affect Reagan's chances in his 1984 re-election bid—Lebanon at the time seemed to be the only issue that could derail him—led to the "redeployment offshore" of the marines, a euphemism for "let's beat a hasty retreat!" The decision to withdraw American forces effectively ended the Reagan administration's "commitment" to the stabilization of Lebanon.[44]

Once the Marines were safely offshore, the *USS New Jersey*'s 16-inch guns were ordered to shell the defenseless mountain villages behind Beirut.[45] This decision characterized the frustration and incomprehension with which the administration had acted in Lebanon. Nothing has contributed more to the violent anti-American sentiment that exists today in Lebanon.

Between 1984 and 1987, Washington almost completely ignored Lebanon, as its many factions bloodied themselves with the encouragement of their respective regional patrons, Israel, Syria, and Iran. The Reagan administration's single concern was to secure the release of the Americans taken hostage in Beirut in the aftermath of the withdrawal from Lebanon, but, as we now know, it sought Iran's assistance rather than directly involving itself in Lebanon again. Only in its last year in office did the administration finally come to admit that little could be accomplished in Lebanon without Syrian support and assistance. Cooperative efforts were undertaken to get a new Lebanese president elected, but, by this time, it was already too late. Had George Shultz and his advisers understood the importance of bringing Syria into the equation back in 1983, Lebanon might have had an opportunity for stability (some might say "survival").

THE REAGAN ADMINISTRATION AND
THE PALESTINIANS

Between 1984 and the end of 1987, the Reagan administration took little interest in the Arab-Israeli conflict, other than to watch from afar a good deal of shadow dancing between Jordan and the PLO as King Hussein unsuccessfully tried to put Jordan forward as a viable representative of the Palestinians in future negotiations with Israel. A number of factors were behind the failure of Hussein's approach, but ultimately it was doomed because the Reagan administration was unwilling at the time to become a full partner in a peace process: Reagan did not want to become personally involved, Shultz was still stewing over the Lebanon fiasco and felt that Arab leaders could not be trusted and "were unreliable as potential partners in a complex negotiation," and White House advisers counseled that opposition in Israel to the Jordanian option was too pronounced to warrant risking a breach of the U.S.-Israeli relationship.[46] After King Hussein's failure to convince Washington to conduct exploratory meetings with a joint Jordanian-Palestinian delegation, his accord with Yasser Arafat began to unravel over issues of structure and process. In one short year, the accord had disintegrated, much to the delight of Syria, which opposed it from the outset because it did not call for an international conference, the only framework likely to afford the Asad regime the opportunity of negotiating a return of the Israeli-annexed Golan Heights and influencing the final outcome of the peace process.

One product of the failed Jordanian initiative was an improvement in Syrian-Jordanian relations at the expense of the PLO, which had been engaged in verbal and military warfare with the Syrians in Lebanon and between PLO headquarters in Tunis and

Damascus since 1982. In fact, King Hussein's next diplomatic initiative was to pursue the idea of an international conference that would involve Israel and Jordan, but not the PLO, and that would have the support of both Washington and Moscow. Within Israel, new Foreign Minister Shimon Peres—he had exchanged jobs with Yitzhak Shamir who became prime minister as part of the Labor-Likud political arrangement by which Israel had been governed since 1984—was receptive to the idea of an international conference as an umbrella for direct bilateral negotiations. Shamir and other Likudniks were adamantly opposed, however, to Peres' efforts and discouraged George Shultz from pressing for an international conference.[47]

It would take the Palestinian *intifada* that erupted in December 1987 to revive Reagan administration interest in the Arab-Israeli conflict. The structural causes of the *intifada* will be examined by historians for years to come, especially in light of the fact that for the previous twenty years the Palestinian resistance to Israeli occupation was viewed as at its most sporadic and generally passive.[48] Some of the contributing factors included the worsening economic recession throughout the Middle East, which made life increasingly difficult for the Palestinians under occupation; a growing Palestinian fear that the Arab states were turning their back on the Palestinians because of their own domestic problems and the threat of the Iran-Iraq war (this fear was heightened by the Arab summit meeting in Amman in November 1987 where Palestinian issues were scarcely discussed); and a general frustration that neither Likud nor Labor in Israel was willing to think of Palestinian self-rule in the territories. Indeed, all indications were that the very best the Palestinians under occupation could hope for was some kind of Israeli-Jordanian cooperation in the control of the West Bank and Gaza; for the Palestinians that was simply intolerable.

The uprising soon made it clear that Palestinian rocks and molotov cocktails would not elicit a gentle Israeli response. American television coverage of the violence inflicted by Israeli forces on Palestinian youngsters was particularly graphic. American public opinion, even in the American Jewish community, was unusually critical of Israel. Pressures on the Reagan administration to respond to the events mounted.

The uprising had an especially important effect on Shultz, who had spent the previous three years paralyzed by the Lebanon disaster. Because he had taken personally the humiliation suffered by the administration in 1983–84, it came as a great surprise to everyone when he personally undertook the most important peace overture since the Reagan plan of 1982. He called for an international conference to be followed by negotiations between an Israeli delegation and a joint Jordanian-Palestinian delegation in which the United States would participate.[49]

Once again, however, the Reagan administration's return to peace making seemed to be a nonstarter, despite Shultz's surprising burst of diplomatic energy, reminiscent of Kissinger's shuttle diplomacy in the mid-1970s. Prime Minister Shamir, in typical fashion, rejected the proposals outright. The PLO was angry because there was still to be no place for its representatives, despite the general recognition that its popular following among Palestinians inside the Occupied Territories and in the Palestinian diaspora was unrivaled. And King Hussein, although initially receptive, eventually withdrew from the discussion with Washington at the end of July 1988, reluctantly asserting that the Palestinians had to be represented by their legitimate leaders—the PLO. By autumn, events seemed to have already overtaken Reagan administration thinking on the Palestinian dimension of the Arab-Israeli conflict. Not only was there no end in sight to the uprising, but also the PLO leadership was willing to make the kind of public declarations and guarantees that the Reagan administration demanded: recognition of Israel's legitimate existence and an end to terrorism.

International and domestic pressures on Washington to begin talking to the PLO increased throughout the fall. Divisions in the administration began to surface. The wing that felt strongest about the strategic alliance with Israel had by now lost ground in the wake of the Iran-Contra revelations; those officials who survived the scandal also had to reckon with the reality that the uprising in the West Bank and Gaza was a movement that the Israeli army could not extinguish. The pending Arafat visit to New York to address the United Nations only widened the rift in the administration, especially when Shultz decided to deny Arafat a visa to enter the United States. Shultz's inflexibility, which may have been personally motivated and which inconvenienced the membership of the United Nations, concentrated even more international attention on Arafat. The General Assembly had to be moved to Geneva. Arafat's speech there in December 1988 and his press conference afterward, when he reaffirmed the PLO's recognition of Israel and an end to terrorism, made it difficult for the Reagan administration to hold out any longer. In a turnabout, Shultz announced that the United States would enter into a "substantive dialogue" with the PLO, thereby reversing a policy established in 1975 by Henry Kissinger.

CONCLUSION

In certain ways, Ronald Reagan's Middle East policy followed paths that had already been created in the last eighteen months of the Carter presidency. In the Persian Gulf, his administration accelerated Carter's interventionist policy, but not with any consistency. It moved from a position of neutrality to an official tilt toward Iraq, whereas it surreptitiously made overtures to Iran, and finally, as a result of Iran-Contra, it turned against Iran completely. Apart from lowering the administration's credibility and prestige at home and abroad and creating paralysis at the White House, the Iran-Contra revelations "left its antiterrorist policy in tatters."[50] Yet, the administration was able to preserve American interests in the Persian Gulf because of Iran's failure to win the war against Iraq. At the same time, the Soviet decision to reduce its activities in the Middle East, including the withdrawal from Afghanistan, certainly helped the administration to land on its feet, even it if was a wobbly landing. However, America's seemingly two-faced policy toward Iran and its unwillingness to satisfy Arab requests for arms encouraged moderate Arab states to turn toward Europe for their military equipment and to develop closer ties with the Soviet Union.

It is perhaps too early to estimate the extent of damage caused by America's loss of credibility with the moderate Arabs. Indeed, there may not be any sustained structural damage because Saudi Arabia and the other Arab states of the Gulf no longer possess the leverage with Washington they enjoyed in the 1970s, when oil prices were high and Western reserves were low. If the economic trends of the 1980s are reversed in the 1990s, as some experts predict, then the United States may encounter serious difficulties in pursuing its objectives and interests in the Persian Gulf. Therefore, for the Bush administration to anticipate such changes it will be necessary to reconstitute the bonds of trust that were loosened in the last years of the Reagan administration. Much will depend on Washington's contribution to improving stability in the Persian Gulf region and to breaking the Arab-Israeli impasse.

In the case of Lebanon with its direct links to the Arab-Israeli conflict, the Reagan administration initially recognized what its predecessor had discovered: that Lebanon was not an especially vital American interest. But Israel's war of choice in 1982 sucked the administration into the vortex of an unmanageable situation, which it erroneously assumed could be managed. It extricated itself only after completely bungling efforts to stabilize the political and military situation in the country. Its failure to understand the complex dynamics of Lebanese society and the constellation of external forces that helped to perpetuate the war led to a calamitous intervention that created the deepest blemish on Reagan's foreign policy record in the Middle East. Only Israel paid a higher price than the United States for its gross miscalculations.

As for the wider Arab-Israeli conflict, the Reagan administration became involved only episodically in peace diplomacy, briefly in 1982 and then quite aggressively but belatedly in 1988. Its policy of "benign neglect" may also be viewed as a carryover from the last months of the preceding administration when, after the Egyptian-Israeli peace treaty in 1979, Carter reduced his heavy and personal investment in the Arab-Israeli peace process, especially by not pressing for the implementation of the Camp David Accords as pertaining to the West Bank and Gaza.

Some students of American foreign policy have argued that the institutionalization of America's strategic relationship with Israel made it virtually impossible for the Reagan administration to adopt an activist approach to peace during its two terms in office. This was reinforced by the particular moral claims that Israel has made on the United States and by the remarkably strong influence of American domestic constituencies and lob-

bies that supported a strong relationship with Israel.[51] Only un-
informed historians could argue, however, that the institutionalization process originated with the Reagan administration. Its
beginnings date from the late 1950s when Eisenhower administration efforts to build a lasting system of alliances with the Arab
states ran afoul of Nasser's pan-Arabist and nonalignment policies and the new radical nationalist regimes in Iraq and Syria.
After that Israel's stock rose gradually until its overwhelming
victory in the 1967 war, when it soared. It experienced some
fluctuations in the aftermath of the 1973 war, when the moderate, oil-rich Arab states of the Persian Gulf discovered new but
temporary leverage in Washington. But Egypt's removal from
the military equation by its peace treaty with Israel and the Iranian revolution in 1979 enabled Carter's successor to consoli-
date the process of institutionalization by establishing a strategic
alliance with Israel. Prompting the Reagan administration, of
course, was its ideological compatibility with the right-wing Israeli government, and as the Iran-Iraq war and the general economic recession in the Middle East intensified, the substitution
of moderate Arab dependence for leverage upon Washington.

Yet, if all this is true, how can we explain the sudden burst of
American diplomatic energy on the Arab-Israeli front in the last
months of the Reagan administration and the opening of a dialogue with the PLO? On the domestic front, the Iran-Contra revelations helped to discredit Israel's staunchest supporters in the
Reagan administration, providing an unexpected opening for those
officials who preferred greater administration involvement in Arab-
Israeli peace efforts. This, however, was certainly not a major
contributing factor. It is also unlikely that the sudden reduction
in hostilities between Iran and Iraq was significant, though it
enabled the administration to devote more attention to the Arab-
Israeli impasse than might otherwise have been possible. Clearly,
a change in the willingness of the United States and the Soviet
Union to cooperate with one another or, at least, a change in
the Reagan administration's perception of Soviet motivations both
in the domestic and foreign policy areas, was an important underlying factor. The Soviet decision to withdraw from Afghanistan played a large role in easing the confrontational nature of
American-Soviet relations of the previous eight years. Greatest

emphasis, however, must be given to the changes in the local Israeli environment produced by the *intifada,* and to the attention it focused on the PLO leadership's long and frustrating efforts to convince the United States and the international community that it no longer stood for the creation of a Palestinian state in all of historic Palestine but rather for an independent state alongside Israel. Local, regional, and international developments converged in Reagan's second term to produce important lessons that his administration could not ignore.

What were these lessons? First, the Palestinians of the West Bank and Gaza were willing to conduct a visible, protracted resistance to Israeli occupation, something that had not been anticipated by Washington. Second, King Hussein could not represent the Palestinians in any diplomatic negotiations; the *intifada* demonstrated that the "Jordanian Option" was bankrupt. Third, the leadership of the Palestinians inside and outside the territories was indeed the PLO. Fourth, the PLO had begun to adopt a more acceptable diplomatic posture that focused on recognition of Israel and negotiations toward a lasting peace settlement. Finally, the Soviet Union's apparent willingness to assist in the stabilization of the Middle East region suggested that it was no longer sensible to exclude it from the diplomatic picture; the Reagan administration engagement with a pragmatic, cooperative Soviet foreign policy under Gorbachev clearly contributed to this new understanding.[52]

There seems little doubt that the Reagan administration's decision to open a substantive dialogue at the ambassadorial level with the PLO in Tunis was designed to give the Bush administration a headstart in a Middle East peace process. Had President Bush initiated the dialogue with the PLO at the start of his administration, the domestic fallout might have been devastating. Instead, he was freed to pursue an option that his predecessor had created without having to shoulder complete responsibility it if fails to produce acceptable results.

The historical record indicates that since 1945 successive American administrations have constantly had to shift their tactics and employ a variety of means in the Middle East to accommodate the myriad political, ideological, and socioeconomic upheavals experienced by the region over the years. Yet, America's principal objectives and interests in the Middle East have remained stable throughout the same period.[53] In fact, by the end of the Reagan era, the central policy objective of Soviet containment in the Middle East never seemed more attainable: United States access to regular and comparatively cheap supplies of oil had improved considerably; and American markets, though reduced by the Middle Eastern recession and competition from Japan and Western Europe, remained fairly solid. Historians would be obliged to conclude that the United States has been remarkably successful in the pursuit of its main interests, despite the considerable instability and dislocations experienced by the Middle East since World War II.

In the near future, however, historians may no longer be able to draw the same conclusion. For they will be obliged to factor into their assessments the domestic changes that the Soviet Union is undergoing, the loss of America's competitive economic edge owing to the challenge of Japan and a revived Western Europe, the growing efforts of Middle Eastern and other Third World countries to pursue "political and economic policies independent of the great powers,"[54] and the gradual reduction of American political influence around the globe. How quickly these changes will be felt and how well the United States will adjust to them remains to be seen. It would not be too farfetched, however, to predict that subsequent administrations may eventually face more difficulties than did the Reagan administration in pursuing America's central objectives in the Middle East unless they respond positively to the changing dynamics of the Arab-Israeli conflict. A policy of benign neglect can no longer be a viable alternative.

NOTES

1. See L. Carl Brown, "The Middle East: Patterns of Change 1947–1987," *Middle East Journal,* 41:1 (Winter 1987), 36; Anthony Cordesman, "The Middle East and the Politics of Force," *Middle East Journal,* 40:1 (Winter 1986), 5–15; *New York Times,* August 1, 1989.

2. Michael C. Hudson, "United States Policy in the Middle East: Opportunities and Dangers," *Current History* 85:508 (February 1986), 49.

3. On the historical roots of the Cold War, see Bruce R. Kuniholm, *The Origins of the Cold War in the Near East: Great Power Conflict and Diplomacy in Iran, Turkey, and Greece* (Princeton, N.J.: Princeton University Press, 1980).

4. Recently declassified documents in the Foreign Office files at the Public Record Office in London (Kew) and in the State Department files at the U.S. National Archives in Washington suggest that American interests in oil and markets had already begun to attract the attention of the U.S. government during World War II. In this period Washington first began to challenge Britain for market shares as the United States prepared to replace Britain as the major Western power in the Middle East.

5. Although on everyone's agenda these days, in Islam's political manifestations it has never been a particularly useful lens through which U.S. policymakers could view the entire Middle East region. This is largely because several of the most influential countries, in particular Egypt, Syria, and Turkey, have remained committed to a secular nationalist course, despite growing strains of religious fundamentalism in each. And one must recall that until 1979, the Iranian regime also had a pronounced secular orientation. See Philip S. Khoury, "Islamic Revivalism and the Crisis of the Secular State in the Arab World: An Historical Appraisal." in I. Ibrahim (ed)., *Arab Resources: The Transformation of a Society* (London: Croom Helm, 1983), 313–36.

6. See Bruce R. Kuniholm, "Retrospect and Prospects: Forty Years of U.S. Middle East Policy," *Middle East Journal,* 41:1 (Winter 1987), 16.

7. See William B. Quandt, "U.S. Policy Toward the Arab-Israeli Conflict," in Quandt (ed.), *The Middle East Ten Years After Camp David* (Washington, D.C.: Brookings Institution, 1988), 363.

8. Ibid., 383.

9. A former American foreign service officer who served as both Carter's and Reagan's Ambassador to Israel has written of Reagan: "A deeply convinced ideological warrior against world communism, totally suspicious of Soviet intentions, Reagan was the United States' first true ideological president. He saw the world struggle in stark terms: good versus evil, democracy versus dictatorship, allies and friends versus enemies." Samuel W. Lewis, "The United States and Israel: Constancy and Change," in Quandt, *The Middle East Ten Years After Camp David,* 227.

10. Lewis contrasts Carter's and Reagan's management styles vis-a-vis the Middle East. "Carter was quarterback for his Middle East team while Reagan's 'management style was more akin to that of a profes-

sional football team's owner than its quarterback.' " Lewis, "The United States and Israel," 227–28.

11. The strategic cooperation agreement between the United States and Israel was signed in November 1981, suspended a month later after Israel annexed the Golan Heights, and restored in November 1983. Cheryl Rubenberg, "U.S. Policy Toward the Palestinians," *Arab Studies Quarterly,* 10:1 (Winter 1988), 23.

12. Journalists George Will and William Safire were most active in this regard.

13. Although the American Jewish and pro-Israeli lobby did not win all its battles during the Reagan years, it probably never had as much influence as it did during Reagan's first term, owing to his administration's strong ideological affinity with the right-wing government in Israel, its enhanced commitment to Israel through the strategic alliance, and the emergence of AIPAC as one of the most formidable lobbies on Capitol Hill. But this influence may also be connected to a shift in American Jewish voting behavior. For instance, in the 1976 presidential elections Jimmy Carter won 68 percent of the Jewish vote; he held only 45 percent of the Jewish vote in the 1980 elections. Ronald Reagan won 39 percent of the Jewish vote in 1980, an unusually high percentage for a Republican. This meant that in 1980 a significant number of American Jews broke, at least temporarily, their traditional ties to the Democratic party by crossing party lines to vote for the Republican candidate. In the 1984 elections, Reagan won not more than 35 percent of the American Jewish vote, suggesting "that Jews still had a strong liberal-progressive tendency despite the efforts of Jewish neo-conservatives . . . to pull them into the Reagan camp." See Edward Tivnan, *The Lobby: Jewish Political Power and American Foreign Policy* (New York: Simon and Schuster, 1987), 134, 252.

14. Hudson, "United States Policy," 50–51.

15. The Soviet Union has been even less successful than the United States in developing long-term hegemonic power in the Middle East through local regimes. Nasser's Egypt in the 1960s was the most headway that the Soviets made in this regard. On Soviet-Egyptian relations see: Karen Dawisha, *Soviet Foreign Policy Towards Egypt* (London: Macmillan, 1979). As for the argument that the Soviet Union has enjoyed especially stable relationships with Arab radical or socialist states, Fred Halliday reminds us that by comparison the Soviets have enjoyed a much more secure relationship with India, the largest capitalist state in the Third World, than with any Arab state, socialist or otherwise. The movement of Sadat's Egypt in the 1970s toward the West and the direction Iraq has taken since the early 1980s are indicative of the in-

stability of Soviet influence in the Arab world. See Fred Halliday, "The Great Powers and the Middle East," *Middle East Report* (March-April 1988), 4.

16. See Michael McGwire, "The Middle East and Soviet Military Strategy," *Middle East Report* (March-April 1988), 11–17, and Malcolm Yapp, "Soviet Relations with Countries of the Northern Tier," in Adeed Dawisha and Karen Dawisha (eds.), *The Soviet Union and the Middle East: Policies and Perspectives* (New York: Holmes & Meier, 1982), 24–44.

17. Kuniholm, "Retrospect and Prospects," 17.

18. On the "AWACS battle" see Tivnan, *The Lobby,* 137–42, 145–61.

19. See Eric Hooglund, "Reagan's Iran: Factions Behind U.S. Policy in the Gulf," *Middle East Report* (March-April 1988), 29–30. The normalization of diplomatic relations was a clear departure from policy in the 1970s when Washington had tried to destabilize the radical nationalist, anti-American regime in Baghdad.

20. Rhodri Jeffreys-Jones, *The CIA & American Democracy* (New Haven: Yale University Press, 1989), 240.

21. Hooglund, "Reagan's Iran," 29–30.

22. There was a minority view in Israeli policy circles that supported Washington's tilt toward Iraq on the ground that the radical Islam was especially dangerous and that the Iraqi regime had grown increasingly moderate as evinced by its much improved relations with Washington. See Hooglund, "Reagan's Iran," 30.

23. Jeffreys-Jones, *The CIA & American Democracy,* 240.

24. Barry Rubin, "Drowning in the Gulf," *Foreign Policy* (Winter 1987–88), 123.

25. Rubin, "Drowning in the Gulf," 121.

26. Jeffreys-Jones, *The CIA & American Democracy,* 245. North made this arrangement in anticipation of Congress's decision in March 1986 to curtail financial support to the Contras.

27. Rubin, "Drowning in the Gulf," 127. Rubin writes that "by November 1987 there had been more than 375 attacks on shipping, primarily by Iraqi planes and most often against Iranian ships, and more than 200 seamen had been killed. But the tanker war had a minimal effect on the international petroleum market." As for Iran, it had ". . . no interest in 'closing' the gulf—even if such a thing were possible—because it desperately need[ed] open shipping lanes."

28. Hooglund, "Reagan's Iran," 29.

29. The question remains as to how much the Saudi government knew about Washington's covert policy toward Iran given that Saudi officials

were involved in helping to finance the Contra side of the Iran-Contra Affair between 1984 and 1986, and that Adnan Khashoggi, a wealthy Saudi arms dealer with strong connections to high-ranking Saudi officials, organized arms deliveries to Iran. His partners in these operations included two Israeli arms dealers and a prominent Israeli intelligence officer. See Jonathan Marshall, "Saudi Arabia and the Reagan Doctrine," *Middle East Report* (November-December 1988), 15–16.

30. On the origins of the war, see Kamal Salibi, *Crossroads to Civil War: Lebanon, 1958, 1976* (Delmar, New York: Caravan Books, 1976); Walid Khalidi, *Conflict and Violence in Lebanon: Confrontation in the Middle East* (Cambridge: Center for International Affairs, Harvard University, 1979); Itamar Rabinovich, *The War for Lebanon, 1970–1985* (Ithaca, N.Y.: Cornell University Press, 1986); and B. J. Odeh, *Lebanon: Dynamics of Conflict* (London: Zed Press, 1985).

31. Although numerous American banking and commercial enterprises were obliged to leave Lebanon owing to the breakdown of security in the country after 1975, a number of American enterprises had already begun to relocate to the Persian Gulf region before the war in order to be closer to this new and now most important center of economic and financial activity in the Arab world. Beirut lost its pre-eminent financial position in the region and Washington no longer perceived Lebanon as vital to American interests in the Middle East: This reality contributed to the feeling among many Lebanese in the late 1970s that the United States had chosen to abandon Lebanon and its pro-American government for purely economic reasons.

32. The groundwork for the alliance between Israel and Christian rightwing forces in Lebanon was laid between Maronite leaders and the Labor government of Prime Minister Yitzhak Rabin in the summer of 1976 in the wake of the Syrian invasion of Lebanon. See Ze'ev Schiff and Ehud Ya'ari, *Israel's Lebanon War* (New York: Simon and Schuster, 1984), 11–30.

33. Quandt, "U.S. Policy Toward the Arab-Israeli Conflict," 363; Rubenberg, "U.S. Policy Toward the Palestinians," 23.

34. The Israeli government had been looking for a pretext for the invasion and it came on June 3, 1982 when an assassination attempt was made on the Israeli ambassador to London, reportedly by members of the renegade Palestinian organization headed by Abu Nidal. For details see Schiff and Ya'ari, *Israeli's Lebanon War,* 97–101.

35. A total of 1,200 Israeli troops perished before Israel withdrew from most of Lebanon in 1985.

36. Schiff and Ya'ari, *Israel's Lebanon War,* 62–77; Quandt, "U.S. Policy," 364.

37. One expert suggests that Shultz played only a "secondary" role in ending the siege and evacuating the PLO. See Kathleen Christison, "The Arab-Israeli Policy of George Schultz," *Journal of Palestine Studies* 18 (Winter 1989), 32.

38. The texts of the Reagan and Fez plans are reproduced in Quandt, *The Middle East Ten Years After Camp David*, Appendix D and Appendix E.

39. Quandt, "U.S. Policy," 365.

40. The U.S. Marines that had been sent to Beirut in late August to assist in the evacuation of the PLO and to protect the large number of Palestinian civilians who remained were withdrawn prematurely (they had a three-week mandate), thereby breaking an agreement given to the PLO and allowing the Israelis to enter West Beirut in mid-September. See Schiff and Ya'ari, *Israel's Lebanon War*, 250–85, and Rubenberg, "U.S. Policy Toward the Palestinians," 23–24.

41. See Robert G. Neumann, "Assad and the Future of the Middle East," *Foreign Affairs* (Fall 1983), 237–56.

42. Neumann, "Assad and the Future of the Middle East;" Patrick Seale, *Asad: The Struggle for the Middle East* (Berkeley: University of California Press, 1988), 394–420.

43. Neumann, "Assad and the Future of the Middle East."

44. Quandt, "U.S. Policy," 368.

45. William B. Quandt, "Reagan's Lebanon Policy: Trial and Error," *Middle East Journal* 38:2 (Spring 1984), 249–50.

46. Quandt, "U.S. Policy Toward the Arab-Israeli Conflict," 368–72; Christison portrays Shultz as the consummate, compulsive manager who could not quite come to understand that the Middle East may actually be "unmanageable" and who "allowed himself repeatedly to be diverted from the main issue, pursuing tangents because they were easier or closer at hand, and never developed a broad picture of where U.S. interest lay." His tendency to take setbacks personally "brought anger when crises or unexpected twists interrupted the normal course of events." "The Arab-Israeli Policy of George Shultz," 44–45.

47. Hussein and Peres met in London in April 1987 to spell out their understanding of how an international conference was to be arranged. Quandt, "U.S. Policy," 373–75.

48. In fact, Palestinian society in the Occupied Territories had been experiencing considerable changes since the early 1980s; the rise of mass politics and popular organizations had significantly weakened the authority of the traditional political and economic elites in the West Bank and Gaza. Israeli authorities charged with holding down the territories apparently failed to notice these changes in time to avert the uprising.

See Emile Sahliyeh, *In Search of Leadership: West Bank Politics Since 1967* (Washington, D.C.: Brookings Institution, 1988).

49. Since 1982, the Arab states had called for an international conference, and more recently, the Labor alliance in Israel had come to accept the idea as a preliminary step toward direct Israeli negotiations with Jordan. Quandt, "U.S. Policy," 376.

50. Jeffreys-Jones, *The CIA & American Democracy*, 246.

51. Rubenberg, "U.S. Policy Toward the Palestinians," 30–31; Tivnan, *The Lobby*.

52. Another lesson that the administration had slowly begun to absorb was that if it hoped to accomplish anything in Lebanon it would need Syrian cooperation and that this lesson might also be applicable to the wider Arab-Israeli conflict. To isolate and ignore Syria might well be counterproductive.

53. Rubenberg, "U.S. Policy Toward the Palestinians," 33.

54. Ibid.

5

Reagan Administration Policy in Central America

SUSANNE JONAS

In August 1987 as part of the press corps, I attended the meeting where the five Central American presidents signed the Central American Peace Accords. From my perspective as an observer of Central American politics for the past twenty years, the image of the five presidents standing together was dramatic, historic. It represented a striking defeat for the Reagan administration, whose major diplomatic campaign for seven years had been to isolate the Sandinistas from the rest of Central America (while trying to overthrow their government militarily). For the second time in recent history (the first being the triumph of the Nicaraguan Revolution eight years earlier), there was something new in the relationship of Central America to the United States, historically a relationship of subordination/domination. The accords defied the Reagan administration because they implied the beginning of the end of the Contras and the Contra war, the possibility of peaceful coexistence between Nicaragua and its neighbors, and negotiated solutions to the civil wars in three countries. To put it another way, the signing of the accords (referred to in Central America as Esquipulas II) broke the devastating cycle of the predictable and opened up a new process.

A year later, the Reagan administration had found a number of ways to reassert its will and reinsert its goals into the Central American process. As became clearest to me in directly observing the Shultz diplomacy in Central America during the summer of 1988, the United States regained the initiative in some important areas. Nevertheless, I think Esquipulas II symbolizes some of the new realities in the Western Hemisphere, which, along with other factors, shaped the Reagan policy and forced a modification not in its goals but in its tactics. As a result, by the end of the Reagan administration, significant changes had taken place. Where U.S. domination used to be the only (or primary) determinative factor, today there are several conflicting dynamics. The outcome of this interaction is by no means predetermined.

This essay attempts to interpret several issues. First, what did the Reagan administration hope to accomplish in Central America? To what extent was its policy "new," in the sense of representing a departure from the goals of previous administrations? In what respects was it a bipartisan policy, and in what respects unique to the Reagan administration? Second, what were the structural constraints on fulfilling those goals? Third, how did the Reagan administration deal with these limitations? What were the resulting policies, and what effects did they have in Central America? Fourth, in what respects did they succeed or fail? Finally, what was the larger historical significance of this experience?

I develop the argument that, caught between extremist goals and objective constraints, the Reagan administration devised a two-track policy, a "double game," so to speak, which explains some of the apparent contradictions in its policies.

Running throughout this discussion is a basic question: Will the United States permit negotiated settlements to conflicts in its sphere of influence or backyard, or will it keep the wars going? Can it prevent such settlements, given the overwhelming support for them at the level of civil society in Central America? I think the experience of the Reagan administration in Central America suggests that, whereas the United States can no longer *unilaterally* determine the outcome, it does retain sufficient power to veto outcomes that it opposes. In this sense, it is a vast oversimplification to say that the Reagan policy "failed." The future of U.S.-Central American relations and in fact the future of Central America is open; a history is writing itself daily.

Too much has been written about U.S. policy in Central America to summarize here. My objective is to add some observations from the perspective of having studied the Reagan policy not only from Washington but "on the ground" in the region. Since the Reagan administration so clearly focused most of its attention on Central America, that is also my primary focus— though within the larger hemispheric context. In fact, some of the major factors affecting Central America, such as the structural redefinition of the region's relation to the United States, reflect larger processes of change in the entire hemisphere. This structural redefinition was visible first with other Latin American countries (as expressed, for example, in the Contadora initiative).

Whereas many analysts have focused on Reagan policy toward Nicaragua, I look at the policy toward El Salvador and Guatemala as well—first, because the focus of the conflict has shifted from Nicaragua to El Salvador (and Guatemala); and second, whereas the open warfare against Nicaragua never had to happen (and in this sense was a policy choice of the Reagan administration), the counterinsurgency wars in El Salvador and Guatemala are very deep-seated and deeply rooted in post-World War II relations of the United States to the Third World.

REAGAN ADMINISTRATION GOALS AND THE MANICHAEAN WORLDVIEW

The Reagan Central American policy was extremist, not only in its militaristic tactics and adamant rhetoric, but most fundamentally in its goals. Most visible among those goals was the determination to overthrow the Sandinista government in Nicaragua. But this should be viewed as part of an extremist approach to the Central American region as a whole. The essence of that approach was a rejection of all compromise and negotiation, a refusal to permit the belligerent parties in Central America to work out compromise solutions, and in some situations outright sabotage of negotiation processes. The U.S. goal, in short, was *to prevail* over forces perceived as hostile, to defeat those forces, whatever the cost and using whatever means were necessary. This policy was based on a Manichaean worldview, approaching the world in absolute, black-and-white terms (all parties are for us or against us), excluding the possibility of coexistence, negotiation, or compromise with "enemies."

In Nicaragua, the U.S. goal was the forcible removal of the Sandinistas through the Contra force. On the question of whether this was feasible, Reagan policymakers were divided: whereas some believed that the Contras could overthrow the Sandinistas, many others understood from the start that this was impossible. From the latter perspective, the Contra policy was useful in other ways: causing economic chaos and destabilization, destroying infrastructure, and diverting human resources—"raising the pain level," and making Nicaragua a negative rather than a positive example to the Third World. Viron Vaky, assistant secretary of state under Carter, said of the Reagan policy in 1987:

Few people today argue that the Contras can militarily defeat the Sandinistas outright. Rather, the principal arguments have been that a longer war of attrition will so weaken the regime, provoke such a radical hardening of repression, and win sufficient support from Nicaragua's discontented population that sooner or later the regime will be overthrown by popular revolt, self-destruct by means of internal coups or leadership splits, or simply capitulate to salvage what it can.[1]

The Reagan strategy was revealed also in the rhetoric of "making the Nicaraguan economy scream," and "holding the Sandinistas' feet to the fire," all this directed against a revolution that deliberately distinguished itself from that of Cuba, and from the outset pledged its commitment to pluralism, a mixed economy, and international nonalignment. This worldview also led the Reagan administration to deliberately undermine Nicaraguan moves toward greater representative democracy. Further, at no point did the United States accept Nicaraguan offers to negotiate moves toward greater representative democracy. Further, at no point did the United States accept Nicaraguan offers to negotiate about U.S. security concerns.[2] The 1984 Kissinger Commission Report rejected any negotiations that would leave the Sandinista government in power in its existing form. In short, it was not the actions of that government but its *existence* that was intolerable to the Reagan administration.

In El Salvador and Guatemala, the United States was determined to prosecute counterinsurgency wars against rebel forces,
and to see them through to the bitter end, i.e., to achieve clear-
cut military defeat of the insurgents, whatever the social cost.
In the words of Fred Ikle, under-secretary of defense in 1983,
"We do not seek a military defeat for our friends. We do not
seek a military stalemate. We seek victory for the forces of democracy."

In Guatemala this meant a continuation of the decades of
counterinsurgency war begun under U.S. tutelage in the mid-
1960s and support for an allout scorched earth war that leveled
450 villages and cost the lives of 100,000 civilians in the early
1980s. (The Guatemalan war was so brutal that it became the
international symbol of allout war: the "Guatemalan solution.")
Although the United States technically assumed no responsibility, since Congress had cut off funds to the Guatemalan army in
the late 1970s on human rights grounds, in fact the Reagan administration reversed the Carter human rights concerns and urged
renewal of lethal military aid precisely during the worst years of
this holocaust. General Vernon Walters visited Guatemala in 1981
to let the army and the military government know that it was
seen as a "friend." In 1982 President Reagan himself told Congress that the Guatemalan counterinsurgents were getting a "bum
rap," and the administration began rechanneling arms sales and
military aid at the earliest possible moment.

In El Salvador as well, the Reagan administration was much
more visibly involved, and made clear its determination to fight
out the war against the Farabunda Marti National Liberation Front
[FMLN] to the bitter end. State Department officials favoring
negotiations were fired.[3] In this case, millions of dollars of U.S.
assistance and the direct involvement of U.S. military advisors
were required to sustain the war. U.S. diplomats in El Salvador
have argued that they are deterring the real hardliners, the army
officers who favor the "Guatemala solution" of all-out war. But
the bottom line of U.S. policy has been consistent and implacable opposition to any kind of power sharing with the FMLN
(again, a position confirmed by the Kissinger Commission). This
was reiterated to me in no uncertain terms in interviews at the
embassy last summer. Even as all sectors of Salvadoran civil

society (minus the hardline right) came out wholeheartedly in support of a negotiated settlement, the United States continued to oppose negotiation proposals, whether from the FMLN, from the Catholic Church, or from Costa Rican President Arias. The intransigent aversion to negotiated settlements was replicated at the regional level, in the U.S. stance toward Contadora in the mid-1980s, and more recently toward the Central American peace process. As revealed in a 1984 NSC document leaked to the *Washington Post,* the Reagan administration's policy toward Contadora was to systematically block all diplomatic moves that might be acceptable to Nicaragua. The NSC document claimed, "We have trumped the latest Nicaraguan/Mexican efforts to rush signature of the unsatisfactory Contadora agreement. . . ."

Similarly, the Reagan response to the Central American Peace Accords of August 1987 was to view them as "fatally flawed" because they recognized the legitimacy of the Nicaraguan government and the illegitimacy of the Contras. The U.S. worked actively to undermine and sabotage regional negotiations and in Nicaragua the negotiations between the Sandinistas and the Contras. As revealed by Speaker of the House Jim Wright in the fall of 1988, CIA covert activities were deliberately designed to provoke an official crackdown and torpedo the Sapoa accords. To the extent that the Reagan administration occasionally conceded the need for a two-track policy toward Nicaragua, the "diplomatic track" was a thin veil for continuing to wage war (e.g., by making demands known to be completely unacceptable to Nicaragua, and mobilizing the other Central American governments for a diplomatic "declaration of war"). As we see below, this became very evident in the Shultz diplomacy of summer 1988.

Although opposing negotiated settlements, the Reagan administration promoted an unprecedented military build-up, especially in Honduras and El Salvador. On several occasions (e.g., March 1986, December 1986, March 1988), the United States came close to provoking open warfare between Nicaragua and Honduras on the pretext of Sandinista "incursions."

In addition to being extremist in its goals, the Reagan policy was Manichaean in its absolutist spirit: the issues were over-ideologized, and the policy was based on what one analyst calls "a closed system of belief, not responsive either to counterargument or to contrary evidence."[4] It painted a black-and-white picture of reality so extreme that Jeane Kirkpatrick could attack conservative Carter advisers Zbigniew Brzezinski and Samuel Huntington as virtual fellow-travelers of the Marxists because they subscribed to "modernization" rather than simple intervention as a way to stop Third World revolutions. This same logic produced a hyper-demonized view of the Sandinistas and a variety of Sandinista-bashing that was virtually incomprehensible even to conservatives in Central America and other parts of the world. Certainly it was a stark contrast to the spirit that produced the Central American Peace Accords—the desire, even among political enemies, to find some form of reconciliation in order to end the bloodshed.

Most important, in the Manichaean logic, facts and factual evidence became irrelevant to the argument and were ignored or distorted at will. Distortions of fact are by no means unique to an extreme rightist viewpoint; but in the Reagan variety, the rigid worldview played a particular role in ideologizing reality. I mention here only a few of the most salient examples.

Before, during, and after the 1984 election in Nicaragua (which was recognized worldwide as perhaps the fairest in Central American history), the Reagan administration maintained that it was a "Soviet-style sham." In fact, it was the United States that used its influence to sabotage the election, forcing opposition candidates to withdraw (and then decrying the lack of pluralism).[5] After the election, the United States stepped up its threats against Nicaragua, warning that the election constituted a "setback for peace talks" in the region, and could "heighten tensions" with Washington. As late as the spring of 1988, U.S. State Department officials continued to insist that Nicaragua had not had an election.

A related rewriting of history concerned the Reagan administration's claim to be "promoting the democratic revolution" in Nicaragua through the Contra "freedom fighters." Contra chief Enrique Bermudez stated in 1986 that the aim of Contra military attacks inside Nicaragua was not to foster democratic reforms, but to "heighten repression"[6]—a pattern subsequently confirmed by the revelations of Speaker Wright in 1988.

Perhaps the "biggest lie" of all was the one that formed the centerpiece of the Reagan argument, from the first "White Paper'' (March 1981) to the Kissinger Commission Report (1984) and beyond: The revolutionary movements in Central America were foreign-inspired, -controlled, and -maintained (taking advantage of indigenous misery). This became the linchpin of the Reagan rollback policy, since it linked defeat of the insurgency in El Salvador to overthrow of the Sandinistas—and, in the more extreme versions of "going to the source," renewed attack against Cuba. Materially, this took the form of the thesis of the Soviet/Cuban/Nicaraguan arms flow to El Salvador. All available evidence indicated that the Nicaraguas allowed the arms flow only briefly in 1980 and not subsequently, whereas Cuba stopped such activities in 1981; thereafter, Reagan administration attempts to manufacture evidence of a continuing arms flow were disproven and discredited many times over.

BIPARTISAN POLICY CONSENSUS?

Most discussion focuses on the issue that divided the Reagan administration from its predecessor and its critics: the Contra policy and the campaign to overthrow the Nicaraguan government by military force. This did become the centerpiece (many refer to it as the "obsession") of the Reagan strategy in Central America. Nevertheless, it is important to understand as well the broad areas of consensus underlying the Reagan Central American policies on many other issues. In many respects the bases for the Reagan policies had been laid by previous governments in the post-World War II era. The tradition goes back at least as far as the Eisenhower administration's overthrow of the Arbenz government in Guatemala in 1954, for which some planning began under Truman. More broadly, the Reagan policy grows out of the Cold War practices of the United States in the Third World, and the particular hostility to Third World revolutions, whether nationalist or socialist. In Central America, the counterinsurgency policy goals did not change substantially in El Salvador or Guatemala from Carter to Reagan. The novelty was to link military defeat of the FMLN in El Salvador to military overthrow of the Sandinistas in Nicaragua.

Central to the Reagan approach toward Nicaragua was the neoconservative doctrine that Communist revolutions are reversi-

ble, and that it is the responsibility of the United States to intervene to reverse the tide of history, rather than controlling those
revolutions through means short of military overthrow. Some of
the more apocalyptic neo-conservatives such as Irving Kristol
and Jeane Kirkpatrick even saw this as a strategy for eventual
rollback of the "evil empire" and communism in the Soviet
Union.[7]

Contrary to the charges by Kirkpatrick in 1979 and 1981 and
others on the Reagan team that the Carter administration had
"lost" Nicaragua in the sense of actively ousting Somoza, the
fact is that Carter vascillated and pressured for human rights
improvements for several years, but stayed with Somoza virtually until the end. However, faced with the fait accompli of
the Sandinista victory, Carter did not send the marines to stop
them from taking power in July 1979. For this the ultra-right
never forgave him. Carter compounded his sins in the Reaganite
view by adopting a stance of disguised rather than open hostility
toward the Sandinistas, attempting to box them in rather than
overthrow them militarily.[8]

The other major shifts from Carter to Reagan concerned style:
first, the level of ideologizing policy, the superimposition of the
Manichaean worldview, and the crusadelike quality of the goals,
which made policy much less flexible; second, the extent to which
Third World issues were viewed in an East-West framework;
third, the unilateralism vis-a-vis Congress (including the willingness to redbait and impugn the patriotism of congressional critics); and last, the unilateralism vis-a-vis Central America "allies," in contrast to the Democrats' attention (or at least lip
service) to consultation and "multilateralism."

On matters of substance, the differences were relative. Even
on Nicaragua, Viron Vaky, Carter's assistant secretary of state
for Inter-American affairs, commented, in regard to Reagan policy, "Realistically, there are only two directions in which U.S.
policy can now move—toward containment or toward rollback."
Both of these are Cold War policies, assuming hostility. His own
proposals for "positive containment" were still premised on a
view of the Nicaraguan revolution as a "deplorable fait accompli." Democratic policy on the Contras (particularly among
Democrats not responsible to an elected constituency) was char-

acterized by divisions and vacillation more than consistent opposition.

Throughout the Reagan years, the Democrats in Congress swung back and forth on the issue of Contra aid. Most democrats on the Kissinger Commission went along with the generally geopolitical approach to Central America in East-West terms, the characterization of Nicaragua as "totalitarian" and expansionist, and the call for a change in the character of the Nicaraguan government. Only two of the Democrats opposed continued Contra aid. The 1986 Democratic party policy statement did not criticize the Contra policy and made some statements of support for "authentic democratic resistance movements." Even with the unprecedented opportunity presented by the 1987 Contragate hearings to disassociate themselves from the Contra policy, Democrats declined to challenge the policy itself. They confined themselves to criticizing the Reagan administration's recourse to illegal activities and, above all, its refusal to respect the will of Congress. They only definitively deserted the Contra policy after being faced with an opportunity (and a demand) to do so from four conservative pro-U.S. Central American presidents in 1987–88. Even then, liberal Contra critics always covered their anti-Contra votes with anti-Sandinista protestations.

If the opponents of rollback in Nicaragua hesitated in developing a coherent alternative to the Reagan policy, their record on El Salvador and Guatemala showed even less disagreement. The bipartisan character of the Salvador policy can be traced back to the Carter/Reagan transition year (1980), as Carter moved more and more toward reliance on military involvement. The day after Reagan's 1980 election victory, a group of critics within the Carter State Department issued their "Dissent Paper," warning:

Should President Reagan choose to use military force in El Salvador, historians will be able to show that the setting for such actions had been prepared in the last year of the Carter administration. . . . Various government agencies have taken preparatory steps to intervene militarily in El Salvador. . . .[9]

In its reliance on military means in El Salvador, the Carter administration laid the foundations for the Reagan policy—thus

bearing out Arthur Schlesinger's observation that "It was Carter
. . . who expanded American security commitments in the Third
World . . ."[10] In the early Reagan years, congressional Democrats balked at the administration's desire to send unrestricted
military aid, regardless of the human rights brutalities committed
by the Salvadoran security forces. After the administration secured the election of Christian Democrat Jose Napoleon Duarte
in 1984, however, such objections were withdrawn. At no point
did Democrats in Congress (much less in the party structure)
propose that Duarte be pressured to negotiate with the FMLN.
El Salvador was barely mentioned during the 1988 U.S. presidential campaign, despite the imminent disaster looming there,
and Jesse Jackson's proposals to restrict military aid to El Salvador and Guatemala were rejected by the Democratic party.

In short, in regard to revolutionary nationalism or socialism in
the Third World, there was substantial bipartisan agreement during the Reagan years. Further, some analysts posit, the 1980s
saw a general shift of the spectrum to the right, profoundly affecting the foreign policy positions of Democrats as well as Republicans.[11] With the end of the Reagan administration, even
with the departure of its team of neo-conservative ideologists
from top policy positions, it seemed clear that the ultra-right would
retain a great deal of power in setting the terms of Central America policy, which in some sense they continued to view as their
"preserve."

Other indicators of the bipartisan shift to the right included:
bipartisan acceptance of the Nationalist Republican Alliance
(ARENA) as a legitimate force in El Salvador; bipartisan failure
to question rapidly increasing military aid to the Guatemalan army;
bipartisan support for the "Discriminate Deterrence" Report,
recommending more intervention in the Third World (more se-
curity/counterinsurgency assistance, with fewer restrictions, and
support for counterrevolutionary insurgencies in some situations).[12] A final sign was the willingness of Cyrus Vance, representing the most liberal position in the Carter administration, to
sign his name to a joint article with Henry Kissinger in 1988,
stating in regard to Central America: "Preventive diplomacy and
preemptive reform can reduce the risks of extremist political in-
fection and radical contamination."[13]

STRUCTURAL REDEFINITION AND CONSTRAINTS

The irony of the Reagan policy was its belligerent reassertion of power in the post-Vietnam era of relative U.S. decline worldwide. Additionally, this was an era in which objective conditions in Central America regenerated revolutionary situations much more quickly than U.S. counterinsurgency could contain them. These same conditions deprived the Reagan administration even of the total support it should have been able to expect from its "allies" in Central America.

The post-Vietnam era has brought profound changes for the United States, both in its international position and domestically. The relative decline of the United States, vis-a-vis its allies, meant that the Western European governments no longer automatically supported U.S. policy. By the end of the 1980s, they began developing their own initiatives in Central America. The U.S. economic crisis, particularly the budget deficit, imposed limitations on military spending for Third World wars (despite the political will of policymakers to continue to fight them). Within the United States attention to the harmful effects of excessive military spending on the U.S. economy increased.

Throughout the 1980s the Vietnam Syndrome continued to be important. Since 1979 a consistent 66–70 percent of the American public opposed interventionist policies in Central America, even when conducted by a very popular president, and even when phrased in terms of "stopping Communism" in our hemisphere. As a consequence of public opposition and its repercussions in Congress, the Reagan administration had to channel funds to the Contras illegally. This was the reason for the events that later emerged in the Contragate scandal. Some have suggested, in addition, that the Joint Chiefs of Staff came to oppose Reagan administration proposals for direct intervention in Central America at least in part out of wariness about fighting an unpopular war— particularly one that was likely to last many years (as opposed to the "lightning strike" in Grenada). For these and other reasons, top policymakers emphasized throughout the Reagan years the importance of overcoming the Vietnam Syndrome and restoring bipartisan consensus. Henry Kissinger in his bipartisan report, as well as Zbigniew Brzezinski and others at the time of

Contragate, warned against the disasters of a "paralyzing debate."

In Central America, the most basic reality of the 1980s has been the profound and steadily worsening economic crisis. According to the U.N. Economic Commission on Latin America, it reached dramatic and unprecedented proportions toward the end of the 1980s. "On the ground," this has stimulated an upsurge in popular movements to such an extent that the army and the civilian counterinsurgents were forced to take them into account politically, alternating between tiny concessions and massive repression. In short, the economic crisis has become a regenerator of social discontent and revolutionary conditions. In El Salvador, this took the form of popular organization staging mass demonstrations. And in Guatemala, 40,000 people took to the streets weekly during the summer of 1988; labor and popular movements entered into a stage of recomposition, despite having been smashed several times over in recent years. (Recent events in Venezuela, a supposed model of stability, suggest that none of the above is likely to abate.) In short, the region is in permanent upheaval, with economic crisis as the principal wild card.

Since the late 1970s, Latin America (and more recently Central America) has been undergoing a structural redefinition of its relation to the United States, referred to as the development of "relative autonomy." Structural and political factors such as chronic economic crisis (including a growing debt crisis) and decades of civil war have created a situation in which Central American leaders—even staunch allies of the United States—no longer find their interests coinciding with those of the United States on all issues. They have responded to their own internal necessities. Above all, they are subject to wide-ranging citizen pressures for peace, pressures that Reagan policymakers appeared not to understand. Further, within this context, the Nicaraguan Revolution itself changed the correlation of forces in Central America—on the one hand, providing the excuse for a new U.S. military build-up in the region, but on the other hand, feeding the dynamic of "relative autonomy" at the regional level.

Finally, the Reagan policies themselves had contradictory effects for U.S. "interests." Most evidently, the Contra policy had serious destabilizing effects, not simply for Nicaragua, but also for the surrounding countries. The most graphic example was Honduras, where conservative coffee growers took the lead in opposing the presence and thoroughly disruptive activities of the Contras on their land. These contradictions were among the factors leading the Central American presidents to break from the Reagan Doctrine, accepting a form of peaceful (if uneasy) coexistence with Nicaragua, and petitioning the United States to end the Contra war.

The counterinsurgency policies and the permanent warfare in El Salvador and Guatemala also had more long-range destabilizing effects. For one thing, the popular pressures from below (and from the revolutionary left) were so strong as to remain beyond the control of even the most sophisticated apparatus of repression. Second, and even more important, the inability or refusal of the counterinsurgent governments and their backers in the Reagan administration to make any structural social-economic reforms in either country spelled a future of permanent upheaval. This is in some respects the ultimate contradiction of U.S. policy under Reagan (just as it was of Kennedy's Alliance for Progress).

All of these factors created real constraints on U.S. policy and heightened the challenge to the United States—both the revolutionary challenge as expressed in the insurgencies in El Salvador and Guatemala and the challenge of "relative autonomy" expressed most clearly in the Central American peace process.

"DEMOCRATIZATION" AND THE DOUBLE GAME:
THE CASE OF EL SALVADOR

The Reagan administration was caught between the extremism of its policy goals and very real structural constraints. In response, the administration devised a policy that, far from being simpleminded or "failed," was quite sophisticated: a two-track policy or double game, with one track addressed the constraints (particularly American public opinion and Congress) and the other less visible set of messages to the Reagan administration's "natural allies"—the extreme right in Central America. The ultraright forces in the region were Reagan's "natural allies," above all, because they were the only social forces supporting his Contra policy and determination to overthrow the Sandinistas. The logic of the administration's Nicaragua policy led it to undermine its own presumed allies of the "democratic center" in El Salvador and Guatemala.

This duality ran throughout the Reagan administration and explains the apparent contradiction between the initial Jeane Kirkpatrick argument in favor of supporting friendly pro-American dictators and the "democratization" policy of the second Reagan administration. Kirkpatrick expressed a gut-level impulse in arguing that any anti-communist government is acceptable—in fact, the more effective at crushing communism, the better. This political preference was expressed in her famous distinction between right-wing "authoritarian dictatorships" (which are friendly to the United States and can evolve into democracies) and left-wing "totalitarian dictatorships" (which must be overthrown). Indeed, such thinking led Reagan to support the most extremely repressive governments of El Salvador and Guatemala during the 1981–83 period.

Independent evidence confirms this affinity for Central America's ultra-right. During the 1979–80 campaign, Reagan team members frequently visited both El Salvador and Guatemala, developing close ties with the military and civilian forces most closely linked to the death squads. Their message was clear and was clearly interpreted by the ultra-right National Liberation Movement (MLN) in Guatemala and ARENA in El Salvador as a green light for increasing aggressive activities. The security forces as well got the message that the Reagan administration would not cut off military aid on human rights grounds. These ties were developed to the point that top military officials in both countries stopped dealing with official Carter diplomats in mid-1980, strengthened their ties to the Reagan team, and boasted (in Guatemala) of having made a "deal" with the Reagan team for restoration of U.S. military aid. The ultra-right in both countries made symbolic donations to Reagan's campaign and openly celebrated the Reagan victory. Reagan advisers, in turn, referred to these groups as the "responsible right." The sharply increased aggressiveness of the death squads in El Salvador during this period is well documented.

By the mid-1980s, however, this approach had become a serious encumbrance to Reagan policy—above all in El Salvador, where it was essential to get congressional approval for the massive U.S. funding necessary to wage the counterinsurgency war. This problem became the primary impetus for a deep debate and eventual shift by the Reagan administration in the direction of supporting a more moderate, "centrist" government not linked to the death squads and more acceptable to the U.S. Congress. As is well known, the Reagan administration worked actively to secure the defeat of its erstwhile rightist allies and the victory of Christian Democrat Duarte in the 1984 election. Within weeks of the Duarte victory, Congress dropped its restrictions on funding the counterinsurgency war in El Salvador.

Officially, U.S. policy since that time has been allout support for the Christian Democrats. By 1988, however, the Reagan administration was sending conflicting signals, some of which served to empower and strengthen the extreme right. Despite ARENA's indisputable death squad ties, U.S. officials called it a "legitimate" party merely by virtue of its electoral participation. U.S. officials also went out of their way to emphasize the "new, moderate" ARENA, refurbished for the 1989 Salvadoran election (and for the U.S. Congress) with a "clean" candidate, not linked to death squads (despite Roberto d'Aubusisson's continued role in running the party). Along the same line, Reagan policy supporters such as Mark Falcoff argued in regard to ARENA's predicted 1989 victory that "ARENA's advance is in line with the general trend of redemocratization."[14] Kirkpatrick and others echoed the same line after the fact—the idea being that if the elections produced victory for the extreme right, the democratic electoral *process* made that a legitimate outcome.

A further reason was that ARENA (like the MLN in Guatemala) was the only force in El Salvador supporting the U.S. attempt to overthrow the Sandinista government, and in this sense was its "natural ally." Throughout 1988 there were rumors that an ARENA government would break relations with the Sandinistas; and candidate Cristiani was on record stating that an ARENA government "could not live with" a hypothetical policy of U.S. normalization of relations with Nicaragua so long as the war continued in El Salvador.[15] In the ARENA presidency, then, the United States may have finally found its needed instrument to disrupt the Central American peace process. In this respect at least, the protestations of Reagan and post-Reagan officials notwithstanding, the ARENA victory could be an asset more than a defeat—a fruit of Reagan policy.

THE 1988 SHULTZ DIPLOMACY AND THE DESTABILIZATION OF GUATEMALA

The Reagan administration also played a double game in Guatemala—in this case, primarily as part of the effort to change the correlation of forces in the region vis-a-vis Nicaragua. The Shultz diplomacy of summer 1988 made clear that, to the extent that the United States maintained its Manichaean vision regarding Nicaragua, it supported rightist at least as much as centrist forces in the other Central American countries.

While officially supporting the "centrist" Christian Democratic Cerezo government in Guatemala, the Reagan administration long sought to change Guatemala's policy of "Active Neutrality" vis-a-vis the U.S. conflict with Nicaragua. This campaign continued during Shultz's meeting with the four Central American foreign ministers (excluding Nicaragua) in Guatemala in August, the culmination of a two-month U.S. campaign to get the other four governments to isolate Nicaragua. During the August meetings, the United States exerted intense pressures on the Cerezo government, alternating threats of aid cutbacks with promises of new military aid, in order to gain its support for a condemnation of Nicaragua (a "declaration of war," suggesting an armed response to a hypothetical Nicaraguan "aggression").

Although Guatemala (and Costa Rica) refused to sign this U.S. statement and ultimately frustrated the campaign, U.S. pressures did weaken Active Neutrality (e.g., by forcing Guatemala to host the August meeting without Nicaragua). Further, these pressures emboldened the extreme right forces in Guatemala that favored action against Nicaragua. But these same ultra-right military and civilian forces had also been actively fomenting a coup against the Cerezo government throughout 1988—or minimally, destabilization of his government to a point just short of overthrowing it, in order to extract concessions on all major policies.

Within this volatile situation, the Shultz visit became an additional destabilizer. During the two weeks following that August 1 meeting, the country was rocked by coup tremors. Certainly if there had been a coup, the United States would have condemned it; but to many close observers in Guatemala at the time, it seemed evident that U.S. policy was effectively undermining the Christian Democrats.

The dynamics of the Shultz visit were particularly volatile in the Guatemalan context because they rekindled the debate within the army (which remains the real power in Guatemala), between the proponents of Active Neutrality and those who saw it as inconsistent with antisubversive policies at home (the latter group tending also to be the golpistas in Guatemala). In short, U.S. maneuvering had the effect of playing to doubts within the military, and in this sense further undermining moderate centrist or democratic forces.

Nor was this an isolated instance of the United States sending "double messages" to the Latin American military establishments. During the years of the scorched earth war in Guatemala, the Reagan administration approved of all antisubversive activities, no matter how "dirty," if effective. The same was true in Argentina: while speaking the language of human rights and democracy to Congress, the Reagan administration was pushing for military aid and training "for even the most egregious human rights offenders."[16] In the Argentine case, the dirty warriors also lent their services for training the Contras.

This record of double messages raises a profound question about the U.S.-maintained counterinsurgency war in El Salvador. U.S. Embassy officials have portrayed themselves as the last line of defense against the "real hardliners" (proponents of the "Guatemala solution" in the Salvadoran army), hinting darkly at a bloodbath if the United States were to withdraw or cut back on its support to the Salvadoran army. One has to wonder whether the United States hasn't been sending a mixed message here, where the stakes are so high, as much as in other countries.

To summarize: These examples of the Reagan administration's double game do not stem from an abstract conspiracy theory, but from direct observation of ground-level realities in the region.[17] The Shultz diplomacy provided a useful glimpse into the many different ways in which U.S. policies and subliminal messages affect the internal balance of forces in the region. Certainly, it is a reminder not to take pious policy statements at face value, when there are so many different levels of political activity "on the ground."

A PRELIMINARY BALANCE SHEET

Did the Reagan policy fail in Central America? Yes and no. Yes, because it failed to stop the march of history, the task set by Kirkpatrick and by Reagan himself. The Nicaraguan Revolution survived the Reagan assault and remained in power. In other countries, both the political solutions (e.g., democratization and the Christian Democratic experiment in El Salvador and Guatemala) and the military solutions (counterinsurgency and counterrevolutionary insurgency wars, strengthening armies, etc.) put forth by the Reagan administration have in some sense slowed down revolutionary processes—this is surely the case in El Salvador—but in no way have they reversed them. Central America today is much riper for profound change than in 1981, because of the relentless economic crisis and the failure to develop reformist policies even remotely capable of addressing the structural problems, debt crisis, or growing poverty. This is the ultimate answer to claims of having made slow but steady progress and "democratization." Finally, the United States was unable by the end of the Reagan years to undo or stop completely the Central American peace process which reflected at least a limited "relative autonomy"—surely a "failure" in terms of Reagan policy goals.

On the other hand, the Reagan administration could count a number of negative successes. It caused extreme damage to the Nicaraguan economy, and hence reduced Nicaragua's appeal as an example to other revolutionary movements. It kept the war going in El Salvador. This is a war that the United States cannot win (in terms of the Salvadoran army being defeated outright by the FMLN). Top U.S. officials appear to believe that the longer they can keep the war going, the more favorable the outcome to them.[18] Militarily, as a result of the massive build-up of arms and U.S. bases in the region (especially in Honduras), the United

States is far more ready to take military action today than it was in 1981. In general, the Reagan administration was able to "raise the pain level" to leftist movements in Central America, although the real price was paid by the Central American people. The wars of the last decade have cost well over a quarter of a million civilian lives in Guatemala, El Salvador, and Nicaragua. Finally, some of the fruits of Reagan policies may yet be seen in the post-Reagan era (e.g., the ARENA victory and a general shift to the right in regional governments, a brake on the regional peace process).

Domestically, the Reagan administration's efforts to overcome the Vietnam Syndrome were unsuccessful, but it is possible that they will bear fruit in the post-Reagan era. Having been unable to change American public opinion, policymakers have found new ways to *ignore* it in regard to interventions in the Third World; at least this is the possibility that emerges from a reading of *Discriminate Deterrence*. In these respects, then, it may well turn out that the Reagan administration has made progress toward reconstituting the U.S. ability to intervene in the Third World and toward removing or getting around the constraints that so frustrated the Reagan administration itself.

But that is all a calculus within the Reagan logic. Let us try to step outside that logic for a final note, a more historical view of the Reagan policy within the context of the bipartisan Cold War foreign policy tradition of which it is part. Guatemala symbolizes, in many respects, the long-range consequences of an interventionist policy. After the 1954 CIA intervention there to oust nationalist democratic president Arbenz—unquestionably a U.S. foreign policy success in terms of its immediate goals—Vice President Nixon visited Guatemala and declared: "This is the first instance in history where a Communist government has been replaced by a free one. The whole world is watching to see which does a better job."

We know now that the legacy of that intervention has been a thirty-year counterinsurgency war—Latin America's longest, and in many ways its dirtiest, war. Even today, after nearly 200,000 civilian casualties, the United States and the Guatemalan army are no closer to "pacifying" the country on a lasting basis. The people of Guatemala meanwhile live in much worse conditions than ever: 80 percent of the population lives below the poverty line. These conditions have continually regenerated social crises and have kept social revolution on the agenda.

But let us suppose that the Eisenhower administration had decided to leave the Arbenz government in place in 1954. What would have ensued? Not communism, but capitalist industrialization and modernization. Land reform had to be part of that process, but it would have served primarily to rationalize Guatemalan capitalism, to stabilize the country by bringing its dispossessed majority into the economy. Not only Guatemala, but perhaps all of Central America might have undergone a nonviolent modernization process, if the Guatemalan example had been permitted to survive, and even to spread.

To return to our starting point: the real issue that faced the Reagan administration and faces post-Reagan U.S. policymakers in Central America is the need to make concessions to change in the Third World. And the first test for the United States will be whether it allows the Central Americans to negotiate political settlements to the wars plaguing them, or whether it pursues the Reagan course waging endless counterrevolutionary dirty wars.

NOTES

1. Viron Vaky, "Positive Containment in Nicaragua," *Foreign Policy,* Fall 1987, 45.

2. William LeoGrande, "Rollback or Containment," *International Security,* Fall 1986.

3. Barbara Epstein, "The Reagan Doctrine and Right-Wing Democracy," *Socialist Review,* Jan.-Mar. 1989, 15–16.

4. Lawrence Whitehead, "Explaining Washington's Central America Policy," *Journal of Latin American Studies,* Nov. 1983, 355.

5. Roy Gutman, *Banama Diplomacy* (New York: Simon and Shuster, 1988); Susanne Jonas and Nancy Stein, "The Construction of Democracy in Nicaragua," in Jonas and Stein (eds.), *Democracy in Latin America: Visions and Realities* (Bergin & Garvey, forthcoming).

6. *Washington Post National Weekly,* March 28, 1987.

7. Irving Kristol, "Coping with an Evil Empire," *Wall Street Journal,* December 17, 1985; Jeane Kirkpatrick, "Dictatorships and Double Standards," *Commentary,* Nov. 1979, and "U.S. Security and Latin America," *Commentary,* Jan. 1981.

8. Susanne Jonas, "The Nicaraguan Revolution and the Reemerging Cold War," in Thomas Walker (ed.), *Nicaragua in Revolution* (New York: Praeger, 1982).

9. "The Dissent Paper on El Salvador and Central America," DOS (Dept. of State, unofficial document), Nov. 6, 1980.

10. Whitehead, "Explaining Washington's Central America Policy," 329–30.

11. Thomas Bodenheimer and Robert Gould, *Rollback: Right-Wing Power in U.S. Foreign Policy* (Boston: South End, 1989).

12. *Discriminate Deterrence: Report of the Commission on Integrated Long-Term Strategy* (January 1988).

13. Henry Kissinger and Cyrus Vance, "Bipartisan Objectives for American Foreign Policy," *Foreign Affairs*, Summer 1988.

14. Marc Falcoff, "Making Central America Safe for Communism," *Commentary*, June, 1988, 78.

15. *Human Events*, Dec. 10, 1988.

16. Martin Edwin Andersen, "The Military Obstacle to Latin Democracy," *Foreign Policy*, Winter 1988–89, 101.

17. On Washington's "ambidextrous" policy, see also Edelberto Torres Rivas, "Centroamerica: La Transicion Autoritaria hacia la Democracia," *Polemica* #4, Jan.-Apr. 1988.

18. Alvin H. Bernstein and Col. John Waghelstein, "How to Win in El Salvador," *Policy Review*, Winter 1984.

6

The Reagan Era in Africa

ROBERT I. ROTBERG

The Reagan administration's approach to foreign policy was decidedly globalist. It focused far less on regional issues than it did on countering the evil urges of the Soviet Union. For that reason Africa was regarded inherently as of limited strategic importance to the United States, and the African issues and concerns that preoccupied the decision makers in Washington during the Reagan years were ones that fitted into a global context or were related to strategic initiatives elsewhere. Africanists and regionalists might have preferred a closer attention to and consideration of the intrinsic policy problems of sub-Saharan Africa, like that of President Jimmy Carter, but crises of world order continually crowded Africa out of the minds of the White House and much of official Washington.

Reaganites perceived African problems to be less critical than those in the Middle East or in Europe. Moreover, the Reagan administration, unlike most of its predecessors, had an unusually bifurcated view of Africa. For the White House and even for the upper echelons of the State Department, the problems of South Africa and Namibia/Angola overwhelmingly were of foremost concern. The resources and energies of the African bureau were focused by the assistant secretary on the segment—southern Africa—which he knew best. The rest of the continent, except for globally related flurries of interest in Libya, Morocco, the Horn of Africa, or special, episodic country-specific conditions, was given secondary consideration. To say that Assistant Secretary of State Chester A. Crocker and his subordinates ignored black Africa would be too strong. Nevertheless, by and large Africans felt neglected throughout the first two-thirds of, if not the entire Reagan administration, and their opinions in international forums were certainly derided in private.

Largely because the Reagan administration's Africa policy was a Southern African, even a Namibian policy, in concept, it lurched from disaster to disaster before finally being crowned with a success. The legacy of eight years must be judged overwhelmingly negative, especially if positive results should be equated with Africa's economic growth, the lessening of tyranny, the spread of human rights, and a retreat from apartheid in the south. There was one grand, almost redeeming, exception. Only in the contested corner of southern Africa known as Namibia/Angola, and only in the final months of the Reagan era, could the United States claim to have helped improve the lot of Africans. Whether or not the Namibian/Angolan peace initiative succeeds, single-minded persistence managed after eight years to bring about meaningful change at the eleventh hour.

"CONSTRUCTIVE ENGAGEMENT" IN SOUTHERN AFRICA

The American breakthrough in the long-standing Namibian/ Angolan negotiations was the only significant positive result of an approach to southern Africa known as constructive engagement. Crocker outlined constructive engagement in *Foreign Affairs* in late 1980, immediately before he was named assistant secretary.[1] It was conceived in reaction to what Crocker and other Republicans saw as the major failure of the Carter administration in Africa: Crocker believed that Carter and company had pushed the ruling white minority in South Africa too hard. Change in South Africa—the reform of apartheid—and the transfer of power in Namibia from South Africa to the United Nations could only be achieved, Crocker asserted, if the United States empathized with the white minority, provided real incentives, and refused to join those who would isolate and castigate South Africa. Whereas the Carter administration threatened sanctions, Reagan and Crocker were openly opposed to sanctions and other measures to coerce white South Africa. Rejecting the arm-twisting tactics of its predecessor, Reagan instead offered South Africa sugar-coated carrots. Whereas the Carter administration was outspokenly antagonistic to apartheid, the Reagan White House and the State Department were gentle, hoping to attract the flies of Afrikanerdom with honey.

Policymaking is not always influenced by rational choice, by informed analyses, or—in the United States—by strategic designs developed by experienced civil servants. Indeed, from his election onward, the stance of the Reagan administration toward South Africa was largely developed and articulated by and in the White House. That informal but formative approach often contradicted or confused the State Department's comprehensively expressed policy of constructive engagement; without necessarily wanting to do so, the White House in the early Reagan years regularly undercut the State Department. By tilting openly toward white South Africa, the White House emasculated whatever sting constructive engagement might have had and vitiated the confidence in American intentions that had been built up painfully and laboriously among the Front Line states of black Africa during the Carter administration.

President Carter and Ambassadors Andrew Young and Donald McHenry, his chief emissaries to Africa, clearly supported the aspirations of black Africa, viewed continued apartheid as the enemy of human rights, doubted the sincerity of Pretoria's intentions regarding reform, and were bold and forceful in their private and public dealings with the minority government of South Africa. Their associates, the ambassadors to and other negotiators with South Africa, were equally unambiguous in condemning apartheid, demanding negotiations with fully representative black South Africans, and in advancing the case of the United Nations in Namibia. Young and McHenry created the Contact Group—official representatives of West Germany, France, Britain, Canada, and the United States—to ensure multilateral support for and coordination of the American approach. Young and

McHenry, and the members of the Contact Group, orchestrated their activities with the Front Line states and with the leaders of the Organization of African Unity, especially Nigeria.

White South Africa, first under Prime Minister John Vorster and then under Prime Minister (subsequently president) Pieter Willem Botha, harbored no illusions of American intentions; sanctions were an option for Washington, and cool, correct diplomatic relations were the norm, with no (or few) special deals for South Africa's nuclear or intelligence agencies. Over Namibia, Pretoria's Ministry of Foreign Affairs knew that the Carter administration was serious in its intentions and that the path to American and international cooperation began with the acknowledgement of UN rights and responsibilities; Vorster made that concession in 1978. Over forced removals of Africans from common land and into homelands, Vorster's South Africa knew that it risked U.S. disapproval. It understood that military attacks on its neighbors also would be condemned by the United States.

President Reagan favored white South Africa. He reminded American audiences that South Africa had backed the Allies against Hitler's Germany in World War II, conveniently ignoring the truth that Vorster and many prominent Afrikaners had been interned during the war for openly supporting Hitler's racism. Backed and influenced in his views by a collection of right wing industrialists from California and Colorado, President Reagan's sympathies were hardly with blacks. When prompted, he abhorred apartheid. It was easy to suspect, however, that he appreciated the anxieties of whites in South Africa and sympathized with their fears that a black victory in South Africa would mean the triumph of godless Soviet Marxism, and would threaten civilization. Accustomed to movie scripts, Reagan saw dark as evil and reacted over and over again during his first presidency to assist Botha's regime. Unlike Carter, he was opposed to sanctions, opposed to the African National Congress (ANC) because it was terroristic, and—unlike his appointees in the State Department—willing to trust white South Africa's intentions over reform, the gradual dismantling of apartheid, and Namibia. He considered South Africa an ally in the struggle against communism.

Reagan's high level of comfort with white South Africa was

evinced less by what he said, although at first he was open in his admiration of the accomplishments of white South Africa, and more by body language, nuance, by what he failed to say, and by his appointments. For the first time, the men whom the Republicans sent to lead the American diplomatic missions in southern Africa all derived from the political rather than the professional sector. Big-game hunters from Colorado and California were dispatched to Lesotho and Botswana, a baby food products heir went to Swaziland, and a corporate official to Zimbabwe. All were known for their family contributions to the Republican party. The political appointee to South Africa was a journalist distinguished by his family ties to other writers and commentators close to rock-ribbed conservative Republicans, and by his forceful advocacy, in the columns of *Fortune,* of the case against sanctions and disinvestment.

Possibly unintentionally, President Reagan communicated a disdain for black Africa by nominating men to the less important diplomatic posts who had no previously expressed interest in foreign affairs and no clear qualifications for important, if peripheral postings on the fringe of apartheid. His political appointments elsewhere in Africa were of the same caliber and carried the same message: Reagan's White House (and his State Department, too) had little time or respect for black Africans, for the OAU, for liberation groups, or for change in southern Africa. At first, too, the White House, the National Security Council, and the voice of the United States at the United Nations were so narrowly and stridently anti-communist that Africa was viewed more as an enemy than a potential ally. The views of Senator Jesse Helms (N.C.), white South Africa's most fervent and prominent proponent in Congress, were welcomed and accepted in the White House (but not in the State Department).

It was with a sense of righteous self-confidence that constructive engagement was put into practice and Washington's break with the policies of Carter demonstrated. Friendly relations with South Africa were reestablished and, for a time, the reform initiatives of the white government embraced, despite a palpable absence of support for such initiatives among articulate blacks. Nicer words and friendlier attitudes led to tactical demonstrations of the "improved" relationship: The United States lifted its embargo on a range of strategic exports, made significant changes in the nature of its embargo on the supply of nuclear fuels, criticized South Africa less in public and in private, relaxed visa and other restrictions, and tried to improve the investment climate.

These gestures were intended by Washington to achieve the retrocession of Namibia and, once Namibia was on the road to independence, to encourage gradual, progressive change within South Africa and important improvements in South Africa's attitude toward its neighbors. Instead, Botha's South Africa heard the Reagan message and responded appropriately. In stark contrast to its behavior during the Carter era, official South Africa took every advantage of the sea change in Washington. Under the umbrella of Reaganism and constructive engagement (and at first with the quiet support of Washington), it lashed out at ANC assembly points and political operations in Mozambique, Botswana, Lesotho, Zimbabwe, and Zambia. It bombed Maputo, raided Gaberone, Lusaka, and Harare, menaced Mbabane and Maseru, and ultimately succeeded in forcing overt ANC operations out of South Africa's immediate neighborhood. South African military intelligence funded Ndebele dissidents in Zimbabwe, organized sabotage squads within Zimbabwe's army and air force, and tried (and for a time succeeded) in other ways to destabilize the new nation across the Limpopo River.

Even more destructive of peace and development in the region was Renamo, or the Mozambique Resistance Movement, which South Africa promoted vigorously. Originally a product of Rhodesian counterinsurgency activities, after 1980 Renamo became an arm of South African military intelligence. Undermining the then Marxist-leaning government of Mozambique was Renamo's function. Funded and supplied with arms from South Africa, it harassed and later cut the government's hold on outlying provinces of the poor and always fragile country. Near the end of Reagan's first term, Renamo was a major contender for power in all of Mozambique; South Africa had succeeded in its campaign of destabilization and disorientation beyond its most ambitious expectations.

The United States helped broker an end to the conflict in 1984. South Africa promised the United States and Mozambique that it would end its support of Renamo (and the United States believed what the South Africans said). But the insurgency continued, with a new verbal protest but little other effective activity on the part of the Reagan administration.

Angola was another area of southern Africa over which South Africa flexed its military muscles under the cover of constructive engagement. In the time of Carter there was a single major foray into Angola, which was condemned by Washington. Beginning in 1981, South African troops crossed the Namibian/Angolan border frequently, at first in pursuit of guerrillas from the South West African Peoples' Organization (SWAPO), later to create a South African dominated buffer zone in southern Angola (like Israel's in Lebanon) and to support the Union for the Total Independence of Angola (UNITA) against the Cuban- and Soviet-backed forces of the government of Angola. For several long periods throughout the 1980s, South Africa controlled and occupied a swath of territory extending 250 kilometers north into Angola. Until the Cubans and the Soviets developed appropriate defenses late in the 1980s, South Africa dominated the skies, patrolled at will, and even installed its own radar on Angolan soil. Meanwhile, supplied and funded primarily from South Africa, UNITA gained strength. It operated throughout nearly all of Angola from bases in the southeastern corner of the country, often dominating about 40 percent of the rural areas of the nation.

UNITA was, by definition, anti-communist and anti-Cuban. UNITA destabilized Angola, contributed to the massive growth of South African hegemony in the region, and helped South Africa curtail both SWAPO and the ANC. It was a prime instrument of apartheid, but the Reagan administration, pressured by right-wing Republicans and the anti-Cuban lobby in Florida, also construed support for UNITA as a useful counter to the Soviets globally. Despite sharp congressional and other opposition, the Reagan administration began supplying Stinger antiaircraft missiles to UNITA in 1986, thus cementing American ties to South Africa in the most open and concrete manner.

Within South Africa, too, the American embassy was regarded by blacks as pro-white or, at least, as being focused primarily on the fortunes and reform pretensions of the National party. In the beginning, too, the embassy was both loath and slow publicly to criticize the government when it threatened and later undertook massive removals of Africans, created the KwaNdebele homeland, attempted to dismantle the KaNgwane homeland, and broke up or otherwise harassed the activities of trade unions and their leaders.

The policy goals of constructive engagement conditioned these American approaches to South Africa during much of the Reagan era. With Namibian independence the ostensible object of American efforts, too much opposition to or protest against Botha's government was believed counterproductive. But as South Africa visibly strengthened its grip on Namibia, Washington gradually began to appreciate that constructive engagement had no teeth. Instead, South Africa pounded away at Angola and other targets, in Namibia installed a succession of hardline administrators who ruled by fiat, eventually resurrected the discredited Turnhalle initiative of the late 1970s, and generally ignored the bleats and blandishments of Crocker and associates.

Only the massive black protest that erupted into violence in 1984 and continued into 1987 matured the approach of the Reagan administration to South Africa. As South Africa's urban townships erupted in late 1984 and youthful community leaders quickly wrested the initiative from white local and national government, so television coverage in the United States intensified American popular and national interest in the problems of apartheid.

Blacks obviously had contempt for Botha's reform agenda. They braved armed assaults and endured beatings, detention, and enforced exile. Their sticks, stones, and Molotov cocktails were no match for the guns of white and black soldiers and police. About 6,000 protestors were killed, 10,000 wounded, and 30,000 to 40,000 imprisoned at one or various times. More than one million Africans ceased paying rent for their little houses in the scattered urban townships, and maintained a successful boycott for four years. Tens of thousands of students boycotted classes and examinations. Three imposed states of emergency, censorship, jailings, the banning of organizations and individuals, and several major concessions, including the abolition of the long-hated pass laws, by 1987 permitted the white government to drive the rebellion underground.

By then, the consciousness of the West was aroused. Leading commercial banks in the United States and Europe refused in late 1985 to rollover short-term loans to South Africa, precipitating the first serious economic threat to Pretoria from outside. Already major American and some British multinational corporations had begun disinvesting from South Africa in response to television coverage of the riots, threatened consumer boycotts, and the sharp slide in South Africa's economy that followed the riots and continued to the end of the Reagan era. After the banks, led by Chase Manhattan, turned against South Africa, companies followed. They transferred their assets to South Africans, Europeans, and Japanese cheaply, and hindered the state psychologically much more than economically.

In late 1986 the rush to leave was accelerated by Congress' public hostility both to South Africa and to Reagan's constructive engagement. The Comprehensive Anti-Apartheid Act ruptured direct air service to Johannesburg, proscribed the import into the United States of South African coal, diamonds, citrus fruit, and most manufactured commodities. Although it affected strategic minerals, like ferromanganese and ferrochrome, not at all, and said nothing about gold, South Africa's premier export, legislatively mandated sanctions had a profound impact on the confidence of the South African business community. Sanctions also signaled the gradual demise of constructive engagement.

After sanctions, the chill set in. Official South Africa could no longer cooperate harmoniously with Americans who would not purchase South Africa's exports and who were prevented by Congress from continuing business as usual. The State Department gradually pulled back, too, realizing that the ruling National party was far more concerned about defending itself against the further right Conservative party in the elections of 1987, and by-elections afterward, than in cooperating with the more and more hostile Reagan administration. The dream of a reformed South Africa and a free Namibia was as distant at the end of 1987 as it was in 1981. The Reagan administration's gentle handling, even coddling, of white South Africa had intensified the immiseration of black South Africans and helped to sanctify the destabilization of southern Africa.

Crocker's grand strategy may have been in disarray, but he never gave up. When nearly everyone else despaired of a peaceful resolution to the Angolan/Namibian war, Crocker persisted in seeking a solution. He was assisted, almost fortuitously, by major shifts in the global correlation of forces and by abrupt alterations at the local level. Mikhail Gorbachev of the Soviet Union had consolidated his power by 1988 and had begun to rout the forces of tradition within the communist party and the ruling politburo. Because drastic reform of the Soviet economy had become a dominant priority, he began to deescalate the rhetoric of the Cold War. He stole a march on the West by offering to and then removing intercontinental ballistic missiles and by slowing down the arms race. He pulled Soviet forces out of Afghanistan, risking a loss of that country to Muslim fundamentalists backed by the United States. Likewise, in southern Africa he deemphasized continued adventurism, signaled a willingness to withdraw from the area if South Africa would do the same, and joined the Cubans and the Americans in favoring change in the region. The Cubans had grown tired of the war, too, and both they and the Soviets were disenchanted with the inefficiency and economic weakness of Marxist Angola. So were the Angolans tired of the economic drain of the war and the costs of maintaining the Cubans and the Soviets. At the same time, both the Soviets and the Cubans demonstrated to the South Africans that they were prepared to reclaim the skies over southern Angola and attack the South Africans with renewed force. At a critical battle inside Angola in 1988, South African troops sustained casualties in unexpected numbers. Newly installed Soviet radar and uncommon aggression by Cuban pilots altered the strategic picture.

There had been additional thinking in South Africa, too, as the national economy continued to sputter and gross domestic product growth rates hovered around zero. The business community had grown anxious, and the government, although reluctant to respond to the imperatives of commerce, had begun to worry about continued high rates of inflation, the paucity of foreign exchange and foreign investment, and the steady and undeniable deterioration in the short- and medium-term ability of South Africa to cope with international isolation, further disinvestment, worsening unemployment, a precarious balance of payments position, and the possibility of renewed sanctions. It made sense for South Africa to find a way to gain diplomatic credit and economic relief by agreeing to cease occupying and attacking Angola. During negotiations in late 1988, South Africa also promised to cease supplying UNITA, leaving it to be sustained by American and some African and Arab support, and to give Namibia its independence. The Cubans agreed to leave Angola over three years. The South Africans finally accepted the conditions of Security Council Resolution 435 of 1978, which committed them to reduce their troops in Namibia to a maximum of 1,500, and to welcome a UN peacekeeping force of 4,600, as well as a police contingent of 800 and an election monitoring group of 500.

The signing of an omnibus accord before Christmas 1988, as the Reagan administration faded away, was a triumph for Crocker. He had brought Cubans, Soviets, and Angolans together in repeated sessions with South Africa to conclude a major treaty of peace. It greatly minimized the threat to white South Africa of the ANC, which lost bases in Angola and had to move to Tanzania, and of the Cubans and Soviets, who began to go home. It delivered Namibia into the hands of the UN, at last, and was expected to produce an election there in late 1989 and independence in 1990, under a black-dominated government. This conclusion, the triumph of constructive engagement, came about because of skillful and persistent American efforts and because the main original thrust of constructive engagement—support for the reform efforts of white South Africa—had produced no meaningful progress at all.

CONFRONTING LIBYA

Libya was another object of the Reagan administration's foreign policy in Africa. Muammar al-Quaddafi, Libya's ruler, had made his country of only four million people a major international nuisance during the Carter years. Whether Libya's anti-Americanism was all pose or not, mobs had burned the

American embassy in Tripoli in 1979. Under Reagan, among Washington's first moves regarding Africa was the expulsion of Libya's diplomats from the United States. "Libya and the world were put on notice that Quaddafi's revolutionary ambitions would not be tolerated."[2] Naval air forces began to assert U.S. control over the Gulf of Sidra, off Libya. In 1982 the import of oil from Libya and exports there of high technology equipment was proscribed. A year later, after Libya supported an invasion of neighboring Chad by Chadian dissidents, the United States supplied aircraft with sophisticated early warning detection capabilities and helped airlift French paratroopers to bolster the defenses of President Hissene Habre. The Libyan attack was contained and Habre strengthened, but for several more years Libya and its Chadian clients occupied a sizable portion of the northern Chadian desert. Libya wanted control over a strip in northern Chad that was believed to be rich in uranium and other exploitable minerals. Libya also sought to show its national vigor.

By Reagan's second term, Crocker and others were active in planning new ways of curbing Quaddafi. By 1984, Libya was believed to be a major sponsor of international terrorism; assassination of its own anti-Quaddafi exiles was occurring regularly; world leaders had been threatened; and Libyan funds were assisting mounting waves of terror by the Palestine Liberation Organization, various pro-Iranian groups, and even the Irish Republican Army. The mid-1985 hijacking of an American passenger aircraft by Lebanese Arab militants, and the seventeen-day ordeal of many of its passengers, infuriated the United States. So did bomb attacks on the Rome and Vienna airports later that year. Quaddafi's direct role in the hijacking and the airport attacks was limited, but his support of terrorism and anti-Americanism was believed to have contributed massively to the attitudes that led to such outrages.

In March 1986 a plan of retaliation had been agreed upon in Washington. During that month the United States began naval exercises in the Gulf of Sidra, including waters claimed by Libya as territorial. Libya wisely responded only very meekly to the challenge, losing two patrol boats. A few weeks later, however, a discotheque in Berlin patronized by American servicemen was blown up; Quaddafi's malevolent hand was seen. Nine days later

U.S. aircraft bombed and strafed targets near Tripoli and Benghazi, and killed two of Quaddafi's sons, although the ruler himself escaped.

The raid, Africa's Grenada as far as the Reagan administration was concerned, led to no destabilization of Quaddafi regime. His army stayed in its barracks and Quaddafi himself, although shaken, ruled with as much quirky authoritarianism as before. International terrorism may have abated for a time, but aircraft bombings and kidnappings in Lebanon hardly ceased, with Syria believed to be the ultimate culprit. Yet the raid did curb Quaddafi in more subtle ways. His adventurism in Chad and the Sudan, and elsewhere in North Africa, was thereafter modulated and moderated. Indeed, with Libya and Quaddafi weakened in esteem by the raid, French-supported troops in 1987 finally ousted Libya from its last redoubts in northern Chad.

The Reagan administration can claim credit for having helped to reduce Quaddafi's influence. Of equal importance, however, was the drastic collapse of world oil prices. During the later 1980s Libya had to pull in its belt as oil prices per barrel fell to a third of their 1970s high. Quaddafi's government was still wealthy, but it was no longer awash with petrodollars. The country's chastened lifestyle thus owed as much to supply and demand as to the implacable hostility of the United States. But Libya's ambitions were undeniably more restrained than in 1981 and for that beneficial result Crocker and Reagan understandably took responsibility.

DIFFICULTIES IN THE HORN OF AFRICA

In the Horn of Africa, U.S. policy for decades had been conditioned by a loyalty to and reliance upon Emperor Haile Selassie I's Christian-ruled Ethiopia. From his heroic resistance to invading Italians in 1936 to his alliance with the West during the darkest days of the Cold War, Selassie had been a key American ally in Africa. Even after the brutal rebellion in 1974 that replaced his monarchy with a junta of Marxist-leaning officers, the United States maintained its ties to the linchpin of northeastern Africa. The Soviets meanwhile backed Somalia, Ethiopia's arch rival. When Somalia unwisely attacked Ethiopia in 1977 with Soviet arms, intending to reclaim the barren wastes of the Ogaden on behalf of Somali national irredentism, the Soviets switched sides, and the United States, without wanting or meaning to, became Somalia's patron.

The United States desired bases along the Gulf of Aden because of potential combat in the Persian Gulf. For that reason, and in order to counter the Soviet support for Ethiopia's Mengistu Haile Meriam, it gave military aid to the Somalis in 1982 and thereafter. The Reagan administration never broke relations with Ethiopia. Nor did it try to give covert assistance to the Eritrean People's Liberation Force, the Tigrean People's Liberation Front, or other opponents of Mengistu's harsh regime. It backed the Somalis, but always with distaste and reluctance. It condemned the human rights lapses of the Ethiopian government, and repeatedly told Mengistu so. But it treated Mengistu far more evenly than Quaddafi and, to the Reagan administration's great credit, the United States was generous in providing food aid for famine relief without making political demands.[3]

In the Sudan, during these same years, an American client and tyrant, Gaaffar al-Nimeiry, was massively supported to counter Libyan influence, but when he was ousted in 1985, the United States did nothing. It also stood by helplessly as Sadiq el-Mahdi, Nimeiry's eventual successor, was unable to govern his bankrupt, famine-ridden, and wartorn country. Crocker attempted on several occasions late in his tenure to help bring about a cease-fire between the rebellious Sudanese People's Liberation Army in the south, and the Arab northerners, but peace in the Sudan was to await his successor's initiative. So was the relief of thousands of famine victims in the desperate southwest of the Sudan.

Under Reagan, the United States accomplished little of positive value in the Horn of Africa and the Sudan. The excesses of its clients, Siad and Nimeiry, contributed to the economic and political decay of both nations. Reaganism, military and non-military aid, and the American naval involvement with a base in northern Somalia led to no improvements in the basic conditions of Somalis or Sudanese. Certainly in the Sudan, Washington had little influence regarding Nimeiry's attitude toward the Christian south. Nor did it influence Siad to improve the lot of Somalis or to disengage from costly warfare against Ethiopia. Washington had no greater influence over the succession of events in Ethiopia. Of potential value to the Bush administration, however, Reagan's team never backed completely away from Ethiopia and Mengistu. When Mengistu began tentatively turning from the Soviet embrace in 1988, American diplomats were still in Addis Ababa.

TOLERATING TYRANTS

Supporting tyrants in Africa was not unique to the Reagan administration. Even Carter, preaching human rights as he did, was nevertheless compelled for global and regional policy imperatives to tolerate if not support a host of unsavory regimes. The Reagan administration (as well as its predecessors) could not find a practical means—even if it had wished to do so—to withdraw patronage from rulers and governments such as in Kenya and the Ivory Coast, which were intolerant of dissent but otherwise pro-Western. Nor did it pay very much attention to the poorest states, such as the Central African Republic and Burkina Faso, whatever the quality of their governments. Whereas the Carter administration kept in close contact with Nigeria, black Africa's biggest state, Crocker (and Reagan) paid it little regard. Possibly its problems were too vast in the aftermath of the oil price collapse. Perhaps, as well, Nigeria was too openly critical of the American approach to South Africa. Certainly there was always a distancing of the United States during the Reagan years from those African nations (the majority) that were critical of constructive engagement.

For the same reasons, the United States continued the policies of its predecessors, remaining staunch friends with President Mobutu Sese Seko of Zaire. Other governments were corrupt, but Mobutu's was more egregiously predatory than most for longer. Washington knew that Mobutu long ago salted billions away in Florida and Switzerland. It was well suspected that Mobutu's wealth could redeem Zaire's national debt of about $8 billion, and restore the nation to prosperity. But Crocker and others were afraid of what might follow his removal. Instability might have posed problems for Zaire and for American's foreign policy toward southern Africa. His big airbase in southern Zaire proved exceedingly helpful to the United States. Mobutu backed UNITA and provided a conduit for weapons destined for that insurgency. Likewise, Mobutu has been staunchly anti-Soviet. Given its global priorities, it is no wonder that the Reagan administration coddled and cossetted the state that probably preyed more exactingly on its people than any other in Africa.

ERRATIC ASSISTANCE

Despite such lapses, the Reagan administration from time to time tried to provide incentives for positive change in Africa. It promised aid to those governments that shifted from socialistic to market incentives for farmers and other producers. It had some successes, too, in encouraging African countries to abandon the policies that had contributed to their economic failures. But, like so much of U.S. aid since the 1960s, assistance to Africa during the 1980s was erratic and episodic. Most of the millions of dollars devoted to Africa was tied to security-related questions. Famine relief was the other large category of expenditure. Proportionately very little was spent during the Reagan years on economic or political development, and what little there was went to a few favored friends—the Sudan and Kenya particularly. Congress never wanted to help needy but occasionally antagonistic governments such as those of Mozambique and Zimbabwe. Even solidly democratic Botswana, in the cockpit of South African displeasure, was treated with equal distaste.

Because the overall record of U.S. economic and political developmental assistance in Africa has been so poor, it would be wrong to hold the Reagan administration to high standards. On the positive side, certainly it did nothing remarkable for Africa. On the negative side, its military assistance to the Sudan deepened the war in that country's south and pushed a rotten regime deeper into bankruptcy. The refusal to aid Mozambique may have made the rise of Renamo, backed by South Africa, a little easier than otherwise. Help for Kenya contributed to the advanced corruption of President Daniel arap Moi and the intolerance of his government. Zaire's people continued to suffer under Mo-

butu. The gift of Stingers to UNITA prolonged a bloody, destabilizing war in southern Africa.

Along with these pluses and minuses must be placed policies
of a macro kind that were starkly misguided and that led to the
continued impoverishment of black Africa. Africa's major mal-
ady is its unbridled population growth. Kenya at 4.2 percent a
year (doubling every 17 years) and Zimbabwe at 3.6 percent a
year lead the pack, but it is estimated that black Africa as a
whole (including South Africa) is growing at rates exceeding 3.2
percent annually. By contrast Asia is increasing at no more than
1.6 percent a year, and Europe and the United States at under
1.5 percent year. Although there is ample land in Africa, arable
acreage is limited and the great increase in black Africa's population from 350 million in 1960 to 700 million in 1988 is the clear
cause of rampant hunger, repetitive famine crises, and the great
fall in per capita incomes in black Africa since 1960. In that year
nearly all of Africa was food sufficient. In 1988 only a few African countries—primarily Zimbabwe, Senegal, and Malawi—could
feed themselves. Africa's very high debt and its low rates of
growth all result from populations that have outstripped all manner of resources. Crowding in the cities, conceivably in the future to be limited a little by the scourge of AIDS, and the destruction of Africa's forests for fuel and new farmlands (forested
areas have shrunk from 36 percent to 3 percent since 1960) may
be traceable to the sheer pressure of numbers of people.

The Reagan administration ceased funding the International
Planned Parenthood Federation and other child limitation efforts. Vice President Bush gave a ringing denunciation of such
efforts, because abortions were sometimes condoned by the
Federation and U.N.-assisted efforts. At the local level, in Africa some help for family planning continued. But the attitude of
the Reagan administration was clear; an opportunity to lead or
back indigenous efforts to curb population growth was missed.
A lost decade obviously multiplied the problems of Africa for
decades, probably well in the middle of the next century.

There were other ways in which the United States could have
helped Africa and been a beacon of light for the world. When
the destructive nature of the great debt hanging over Africa began to be appreciated officially, by about 1985, there was time

for the United States to join France and other countries in forgiving or rearranging a debt problem that is too large for Africa and the individual African nations, but comparatively puny beside the Latin American debt. All of Africa in 1988 owed about $100 billion, whereas the Latin American debt totaled $400 billion and Brazil ($111 billion), and Mexico ($102 billion) each accounted in 1986 for amounts about equal to the total of African's debt. Moreover, the Latin American debt was owed to commercial banks. Nearly all the African debt was owed to international agencies and official lenders, such as the United States, Britain, and France. The debt problem of Africa was therefore manageable on its own. However, it became captive to solutions devised for Latin America also. The Reagan administration rejected the kinds of solutions to Africa's debt problem that focused on forgiveness. At the end of the Reagan years, Africa still looked for an answer to the kinds of debt service ratios (80–200 percent of GDP) that few poor nations could ever overcome. Reagan's men left this problem to their successors.

If the prominent legacy of the Reagan years for much of black Africa was neglect, disdain, misdirected aid, an overwhelming focus on Namibia (which ultimately proved fruitful), and South Africa (which was misguided and deleterious to American relations with the rest of Africa), skirmishes with Zimbabwe, patronage of dictators, and the humbling of Quaddafi, there was one shining triumph. President Reagan and his associates left the Peace Corps alone. Under Loret Ruppe, a skillful, broad-minded political appointee from Michigan, the Peace Corps quietly continued doing what the Peace Corps has always done best. It fostered people-to-people contact, introducing young and older Americans to the life of inner Africa as well as its national capitals. Those Americans—approximately 3,000 in twenty-seven countries—helped Africans learn to farm fish, to husband their dwindling supplies of wood fuel, and to learn English, mathematics, science, beekeeping, and other skills. Some Peace Corps people trained African midwives in modern sanitation practices. Others set up public health centers. Most of all, they were there, helping Africans learn and helping them help themselves. The efforts of dedicated volunteers took American knowledge and ideals into the heart of a continent, and they returned with knowledge of Africa and a profound sympathy with it and with many individual aspirations. Whatever the Reagan era accomplished and failed to accomplish, it at least sustained the Peace Corps.

NOTES

1. Chester A. Crocker, "South Africa: Strategy for Change," *Foreign Affairs* 59 (Winter 1980–81), 323–51.
2. Lisa Anderson, "Friends and Foes: American Policy in North Africa," in Robert I. Rotberg (ed.), *Africa in the 1990's and Beyond: U.S. Policy Opportunities and Choices* (Algonac, Mich.: Reference Publications, 1988), 175.
3. See David Laitin, "Security, Ideology and Development on Africa's Horn: United States Policy—Reagan and the Future," in *Africa in the 1990s,* 209–10.

7

U.S.-Asian Relations in the 1980s

AKIRA IRIYE

What we are being asked to assess is the nature of the world transformation during the Reagan era, which roughly corresponds to the 1980s, America's role in bringing about the transformation, and the impact of the transformed world upon the United States. My assignment is East Asia, which I define broadly to include not only Japan and China but the so-called NICS or the "four tigers" (South Korea, Taiwan, Hong Kong, and Singapore) and the four Southeast Asian countries (Indonesia, the Philippines, Malaysia, and Thailand) that are members of ASEAN (Association of Southeast Asian Nations). It seems to make sense to deal with all these countries rather than just with China and Japan, for, as will become clearer, the decade of the 1980s has witnessed a tendency toward regional growth and definition so that developments within China and Japan have become more closely tied than earlier to those in the rest of Asia.

Indeed, nothing is more striking in recent international history than the phenomenal economic growth of the Asian region during the Reagan years. The Gross National Product (GNP) of the ten countries mentioned above registered a combined annual growth rate of 5.45 percent during 1980–85, higher than any other areas of the world, and more than double the 2.4 percent rate for the United States.[1] Only the Philippines recorded a negative rate of growth (−1.1 percent). Of the rest, Japan's 4.2 percent rate of growth was the lowest, a good indication that it was not just Japan that achieved impressive gains, but the whole region. If one excepts the Philippines and Japan, the eight others' average rate of growth would come to something like 5.4 percent, an astounding performance. Of course, it may be objected that for small-scale economies, which most of these were at the beginning of the 1980s, to increase their GNPs by 6 or higher percentages is not really so amazing; it matters much more for large economies like the United States and Japan to expand even by 2 or 3 percent. Even so, the sustained growth of the Asian countries is an indisputable phenomenon, and it is reflected in the fact that whereas in 1980 Asia's share of world output was barely 10 percent, it grew to nearly 20 percent by the end of the decade. Asian economic power, in other words, doubled in the total world picture in ten years.

The economic growth of Asian countries has been achieved in part through population control and food self-sufficiency (itself a product of growing agricultural productivity), which have enabled them to undertake rapid industrialization. Their industrialization has been export-oriented; high proportions of their manufactured goods have been exported, so that in 1989 the Asian countries accounted for more than 25 percent of world manufacturing export. This in turn helped expand Asia's share in the world export trade, which was about 15 percent in 1980 but increased to nearly 25 percent by 1988. Per capita incomes also rose; in terms of purchasing power, it has been shown that the NICS in 1984 enjoyed standards of living comparable to some of the European countries. Japan, of course, enjoyed one of the world's top per capital incomes, its GNP having exceeded three trillion dollars. It expanded its capital outflow in the form of direct and indirect investment, foreign loans, and tourist expenditures. South Korea, too, was about to emerge as a creditor nation.

All these are impressive achievements. Asia, which used to be synonymous with an overcrowded landmass bordering on hunger and poverty, by the late 1980s seemed to be a region of tremendous economic growth and increasing affluence. Whereas pockets of poverty and underdevelopment remained, there seemed to be little doubt that compared with twenty years previously,

even ten years earlier, the region had gained stature and importance in the international picture because of its dynamic economic performance.

THE U.S. AND ASIAN DEVELOPMENT

How much was this development a product of President Ronald Reagan's leadership? How much did the United States under
Reagan desire and help bring about such an outcome? Or was it
more a product of accident, having little to do with American
intentions or wishes?

It seems to me that the United States was relevant to these
developments in two ways. First, it created an environment for
regional order conducive to sustained economic growth. Compared with the situation before 1980, Asia was characterized by
relative stability, or at least by the absence of serious wars. The
war in Vietnam ended formally in 1975. Although that was followed by Chinese-Vietnamese clashes and the Vietnamese occupation of Cambodia, recent negotiations between China and
Vietnam indicate the possibility that the conflict may soon be
settled. On another front, China and the Soviet Union resumed
serious talks, looking to the ending of the rift that began in the
late 1950s. In the meantime, China and the United States worked
out a close and stable relationship. All these, of course, took
place within the larger framework of the U.S.-Soviet rapprochement, which has replaced the atmosphere of mutual antagonism
evident during the first years of the Reagan presidency. Whereas
in 1981, in the wake of the Soviet invasion of Afghanistan, it
seemed as if the Cold War had returned, subsequent events suggested, as Secretary of State George Shultz asserted in January
1989, that the Cold War may indeed have ended. Even if such
were not the case, there is little doubt that Asia as a region had
become much less an arena for conflict and tensions than a region oriented toward accommodation and detente. Good examples of this included increasing contact and trade between
China and South Korea, personal exchanges as well as commercial transactions between China and Taiwan, and the beginnings
of what appeared to be serious dialogue between North Korea
and South Korea. Although it would be wrong to attribute all

these developments to American initiatives or intentions, the fact remains that the United States was instrumental in fostering an atmosphere of accommodation through its negotiations with the Soviet Union, and that the regional stability it encouraged enabled the Asian countries to focus their energies on economic objectives.

The second way in which America played a role in Asian transformation was economic, and this may have been even more significant than the above factor. For it is clear that without close economic ties with the United States, Asian countries would never have succeeded in achieving such growth. Particularly important was the accessibility of American markets to Asian imports. Already in 1981 the United States showed a trade deficit of $27 billion vis-a-vis Asian countries, or 68 percent of the total balance of trade deficit. At that time, total American imports were around $200 billion, so one can well imagine how important the American market was for Asian goods. The picture was even more convincing in 1987, when the United States bought $105 billion more from Asia than it sold there, a figure that came to about 61 percent of the total trade deficit. In other words, within six years America's net Asian trade imbalance increased fourfold. Without such willingness to buy from Asian countries, they would never have been able to expand their export trade, which was the engine of their economic growth. Until 1985 the value of the dollar was kept high, so that Asian commodities were relatively cheap, but even after 1985, when the dollar fell, it had the effect of stimulating domestic demand, thus causing large quantities of goods to be imported even at higher prices. In such fashion, the United States continued to increase balance of trade deficits. Although there were strong congressional and public voices calling for import restriction, the Reagan administration on the whole stuck to a nonprotectionist stance. To be sure, it worked out numerous "orderly marketing" agreements including "voluntary quotas" on some goods, but they had little effect on the overall nature of U.S.-Asian trade relations. Asian countries have been beneficiaries of the relative openness of the American market.

In addition to trade, the United States helped promote Asian industrialization and economic growth through transferring capital and technology. The establishment of American factories in Asia was a prominent phenomenon of the Reagan years, creating jobs for Asians, transmitting industrial technology to Asia, and helping their trade by the shipment of goods thus manufactured for sale in the United States. Here again, the Reagan administration did not stand in the way of such developments, although it did become increasingly concerned over the issue of "intellectual property rights," itself a reflection of the ease with which American technology was transferred abroad.

Of course, it would be wrong to say that Asian economic growth owed itself entirely to the United States. There were certain indigenous factors, above all the high literacy rates of Asian countries. This is something they owe to tradition; especially in "Confucian" countries such as China, Korea, and Japan, education has been traditionally emphasized, and literacy rates have been extremely high (virtually 100 percent in Japan, 93 percent in South Korea, 90 percent in Taiwan, 88 percent in Hong Kong, 83 percent in Singapore, and 73 percent in China). Industrialization is dependent on an educated working force, and this may have been as important a key to Asian achievements as any exterior factor like American economic ties. Likewise, the Asian proclivity to save has been important. It is well known that whereas in the United States only a fraction of personal income is saved, in Japan the ratio is close to 20 percent. But the situation is even more impressive in some other Asian countries where as much as 30 percent of income is often saved. The savings go to reinvestment and to research and development, with the result that productivity rises and economies expand. This seems to have happened during the 1980s. To such internal factors, one should also add that at least in some Asian countries (South Korea, Taiwan) growing affluence has encouraged middle classes to call for political reform, and that political reforms have in turn been conducive to stability, an environment favorable to sustained growth.

What all these developments indicate is that Asia may have been a primary beneficiary, as well as an example, of what seems to have been happening in world affairs; the primacy of economic over strategic questions. It was not always so; at the beginning of the Reagan presidency, as noted, security issues ap-

peared to be of utmost importance. By the end of the eight-year
term, however, power issues such as armament increases, balance of power, military bases, and alliances were losing their
urgency, and instead the questions of trade balances, outflow of
capital, foreign indebtedness, etc., were considered of even greater
importance. Opinion polls indicated that the majority of Americans felt economic threats to the country were more real than
military threats. Whether or not this was what President Reagan
had brought about intentionally, the decade of the 1980s does
seem to have been characterized by the growing importance of
economic as against military power as an index of national security and interests. In the world at large, too, not just in the
United States, nations would seem to have become more interested in economic success than in purely military achievements.
If that is the case, then the economic growth of Asia during the
1980s was a good reflection of this overall global trend.

It may well be that the Reagan administration was slow to
recognize the trend. Even while it pursued arms limitation talks
with the Soviet Union, it kept emphasizing the need for military
strengthening. Examples are its commitment to Strategic Defense Initiatives or "star wars" weaponry and its insistence on
"burden sharing." Both would aim at persuading Japan and other
Asian countries to spend more on defense and military research.
These steps did not fit into the overall trends of world affairs
and may have given conflicting and confusing signals to allies
and potential antagonists alike. Still, it would be fair to say that
the Reagan administration's continued emphasis on military power
did not prevent the overall growth of the Asian economies.

That, in fact, was the irony. Whereas the United States sought
to strengthen itself militarily throughout the 1980s so as to match
the perceived might of the Soviet Union, Asian countries gained
phenomenal economic successes to such an extent that the "rise
of Asia" became a key phenomenon of the decade. In contrast,
the relative economic position of the United States appeared to
have declined. At least in such indices as balance of trade and
balance of payments, the United States began to run up appall-
ing deficits. For the fiscal year 1985, for instance, U.S. governmental revenue of $791 billion fell far short of expenditures to-
talling $1,003 billion; the deficit of $212 billion (equivalent to 5.4

percent of GNP) being financed by borrowing at home and abroad. On December 31, 1986, total governmental debt amounted to $2,217 billion, or 51 percent of GNP, and 11 percent of it was owed to foreigners. Trade imbalances continued to increase, as noted already, whereas foreign investment in the United States rose sharply. All this turned the United States into a net debtor nation, a situation made worse by the weakening of the dollar after 1985. The value of the dollar vis-a-vis the yen declined 50 percent after October that year, making it that much more expensive to repay debts. In 1988 U.S. total overseas assets amounted to $1,254 billion, whereas direct and indirect foreign investments in the United States reached $1,786 billion. The net indebtedness of $532 billion was an increase of more than 40 percent over that of the preceding year. Japan's direct investment in the United States exceeded $53 billion in 1988, second only to Britain's in value and increasing at a more rapid rate than any European country's investment in the United States.

All these developments led some observers to talk of America's "decline," the passing of "American hegemony," the end of "the American system," and the like.[2] It was as if the U.S. undisputed economic position in the world had eroded, to be challenged by faster rising and more productive economies. Paul Kennedy wrote, "uneven rates of economic growth would, sooner or later, lead to shifts in the world's political and military balances." Moreover, "all of the major shifts in the world's *military-power* balances have followed alterations in the *productive* balances."[3] The implications were unmistakable. The United States was in decline relative to others, and there was no question, in his and other observers' views, that Asian countries were among the rising economies challenging the United States. Kennedy mentioned Japan and China as the next potential superpowers to overshadow the United States. So the picture took on an aspect of a zero-sum game: America's decline and Asia's rise. One could draw the logical conclusion: Asia's rise has been at the expense of America's decline. Certainly, if one focuses on America's huge trade deficits toward Asian countries and indebtedness to Japan, the impression may be inescapable that the passing of American hegemony has been a result of the rise of Asia.

It would be unfortunate if that were the case. If Asia's rising economic power could have been achieved only at the expense of the United States, it would be no cause for satisfaction even to Asians, let alone to Americans. But would it not be equally plausible to interpret the developments of the 1980s as a case of growing Asian-U.S. interdependence, rather than of Asia's rise and America's decline? Has the world not reached the stage where national rivalries and comparisons, though still important, must be coupled with transnational and multinational perspectives? Should one not be talking of Asia and the United States, not as competitors or antagonists but as interlinked, interpenetrating entities? At least the 1980s would seem to have witnessed developments that compel us to see Asian-U.S. relations in this broader framework. In such a framework, the important thing would be to note the overall growth of both the Asian and American economics and to observe how Asians and Americans have come to permeate one another. Their lives, their destinies, and their futures have become more dependent on one another than ever before.

THE GROWTH OF PACIFIC INTERDEPENDENCE

This can be seen in the accelerated Americanization of Asia and the Asianization of America throughout the 1980s. Americanization of Asia, of course, is not a new phenomenon, but rather something that goes back to the missionary and commercial contacts of the early nineteenth century. In the twentieth century, and especially after World War II, American economic and cultural influence, not to mention military power, significantly affected Asian societies. It would seem that the decade of the 1980s confirmed and even accelerated the trend. More students and visitors from Asia entered the United States than ever before. Taiwan accounted for the largest number of foreign students in America, whereas the People's Republic of China began sending some of its "best and brightest" youth to study at institutions of higher learning in the United States. Their number reached 40,000 by the late 1980s. Some of these students would stay in this country even after completing their education, thus contributing to life in America in many ways. Japan had sent more students to the United States than anywhere else, but the 1980s witnessed a phenomenal growth of tourism to such an extent that in 1988 2.4 million Japanese came to America as tourists; one out of every 46 Japanese was in the United States as a visitor. They would return home and become agents of the Americanization of Japanese culture. The impact of American intellectual developments on Asian countries has also been notable. Particularly for countries such as China that opened its doors only recently to American contact, the influence of American scholarship has been nothing short of phenomenal. Chinese scholars in all fields, it would appear, are eagerly reading and learning from the latest developments in the natural and social science and the humanities in the United States.

American influence has also been notable in political affairs. It used to be said that American-style liberal democracy was not exportable, and certainly no Asian country is "democratic" in the American sense. Still, American ideas of representative government, the separation of powers, and, above all, human rights, have seriously impacted on developments in Asia, usually through Asians educated in the United States or Americans teaching in Asia. The 1980s democratization of South Korea and the Philippines, though far from thorough, attests to the enduring influence of American political ideologies. The U.S. government also affected those developments by identifying with reformist forces. Even in Japan, a parliamentary democracy, what Americans say and write about politics in that country affects developments there, as happened when Prime Minister Nakasone was severely criticized by the American press for racist remarks he made in September 1986 and had to make a hasty retraction. The Chinese students' democratization movement that erupted in the spring of 1989 and led to the brutal suppression of June would have been inconceivable without the support and influence of Americans, and without the knowledge of such support on the part of Chinese intellectuals familiar with American political philosophy. In a sense the democratization movement in China is a product of the close U.S.-Chinese contact during the late 1980s, and is likely to reemerge so long as Americans, and Chinese in the United States, retain their commitment to human rights.

American society, in the meantime, has become Asianized, perhaps for the first time in its history to any noticeable degree. Imports from Asian countries, ranging from Malaysian textiles and Philippine sewing machines to Korean automobiles and Japanese semiconductors, became available not just in large cities but even in the remotest rural communities. Japanese and Korean factories employing thousands of American workers were established in the South, in the Midwest, and on the West Coast. Hong Kong money, as well as funds from Japan and Korea, began buying real estate. Immigrants from Asia, thanks to the 1965 immigration law revision, doubled in number between the 1970s and the 1980s, and, to take one example, in 1985, 224,000 Asians entered the United States as immigrants. In 1987, 2.4 percent of the American population was of Asian background, and demographers predicted that if the trend continued Asian Americans would come to comprise 5 percent of the population by 2020.

Reflecting such Asianization of America, and Americanization of Asia, interest in, and knowledge of, each other grew further during the 1980s. Asian studies in the United States continued to flourish, the number of students learning Chinese and Japanese often exceeding the supply of qualified teachers. Young Americans, in turn, went to China, Japan, and other countries to teach English. (JET, or the program for teaching English in Japanese high schools sponsored by the Ministry of Education, sent close to 1,000 American college graduates a year to that country.) In addition, the number of American businessmen, lawyers, and other professionals living and working in Japan and other Asian countries increased rapidly, as did that of Asian professionals in the United States.

All these are instances of Asian-U.S. interdependence, not of America's "decline" accompanying Asia's "rise." If such is the case, then what we are witnessing goes beyond the growing importance of economic issues in recent international affairs. What is happening today may well be not simply the primacy of economic over security questions as noted above, but also the rising significance of cultural issues. It may well be that the world is passing through a phase where purely strategic matters are becoming less significant than economic concerns and that the latter in turn are being overshadowed by cultural questions. Certainly, many urgent problems facing the world today are of a cultural nature: technology transfer, intellectual property rights, the environment, protection of endangered species, drug abuse, AIDS, old age, human rights. These issues transcend national boundaries, and close cooperation among nations is urgently required to deal with them. In such a situation, it would seem that the close cultural ties that have developed between America and Asia are a hopeful development full of significance for the entire world, for if Americans and Asians can cooperate in solving these issues across national and cultural boundaries, they can serve as a model for other parts of the world as well. That, in sum, may have been the legacy bequeathed by the 1980s and, whether so intended or not, by the Reagan presidency.

To conclude, developments in Asia throughout the 1980s have been so impressive that future historians may well refer to the decade as the beginning of the age of Asia. But any such characterization would be deficient so long it did not include the United States. In fact, President Reagan, Secretary of State Shultz, and others often talked of the coming of the Pacific age, indicating that both Asia and America were involved in the transformation of the entire region. To complete the picture, one would also have to bring Australia, New Zealand, the Pacific Islands, Canada, and perhaps Mexico into view. This essay has not done so because of limitations of time and space. In any event, what is suggested by the concept of a Pacific age is regional economic and cultural interdependence in addition to relative stability in terms of security. If this analysis is correct, then we may have witnessed an important landmark in the history of the world. Unlike the European countries, which also are developing close ties of interdependence and integration, the countries of Asia and the Pacific have had no history of regional cohesiveness. They do not share common ethnic, cultural, or historical backgrounds. They represent diverse political systems and economic structures. Pacific integration, even if it should come to pass, would be rather different from European integration. For that very reason, the two entities, the Pacific and Europe, would not, it may be hoped and anticipated, develop as mutually exclusive, closed communities, but interact with one another so as to enhance the well being of the whole world. At the very least, the interdependence of Pacific nations would demonstrate that reduced tensions can lead to economic growth, and economic growth to cultural vigor. In this, the role of the United States will continue to be of crucial importance, as an example of a multiethnic, culturally diverse nation, one that is keenly interested in relating itself to the rest of the world.

When "Japan bashing," presidential trips to China, the downing of a Korean plane, and similar incidents are long forgotten, the intensified Americanization of Asia and the steady Asianization of America are likely to be remembered as landmark developments of the 1980s. If so, the Reagan administration will have bequeathed something lasting to the future world.

NOTES

1. All statistical information in this essay is taken from the following two publications: Pacific Basin Institute, ed., *Pacific Basin 1988* (Santa Barbara, 1988); United States Congress, Committee on Ways and Means, *East Asia: Challenges for U.S. Economic and Security Interests in the 1990's* (1988).

2. Paul Kennedy, *The Rise and Fall of the Great Powers* (New York: Random House, 1987); Robert Gilpin, *The Political Economy of International Relations* (Princeton, N.J.: Princeton University Press, 1987); David P. Calleo, *Beyond American Hegemony* (New York: Basic Books, 1987).

3. Kennedy, *Rise and Fall*, 436–37, 439.

8

Reagan and the World:
A Roundtable Discussion

The "Reagan and the World" symposium's final session provided an opportunity for the participating scholars to engage in
informal dialogue, react to each other's assessments of the Reagan presidency, comment on common themes, and elaborate on
additional features of United States foreign relations in the 1980s.

David Kyvig. We've heard a great deal from the press over the
last few years about Ronald Reagan as a great communicator.
The journalistic perception of Ronald Reagan and his administration may not always square with the historian's perception.
Did Ronald Reagan, in dealing with international relations, say
what he knew? Did he know what he said? And did his international audience understand his message? Did they believe it and
did they accept it? In other words, in dealing with the world,
was Ronald Reagan a great communicator?

John Gaddis. I think he did most of the time say what he meant
to say. Not everybody believed him; not everybody took him
seriously; not everybody took him literally. The key to understanding him is to take what he said pretty literally since he was
a rather simple person. It's unlikely that there were the depths
of subtlety that you would find in someone like Henry Kissinger
who might well be capable of saying something for one audience

and meaning something for a different audience at the same time. That's unlikely to have been the case with Mr. Reagan. Careful attention to what he said—particularly moving beyond what the press choose to focus on at any one time but getting back to what he said, which is sometimes quite different from what the press focused on—would be a rewarding thing for historians to do.

Akira Iriye. In the Asian context, the question would be whether Asian leaders believed in Reagan, believed in what he said. Again it's very difficult to generalize because I talked about ten different countries in Asia. There would be ten different answers. I think much of the Asian response may have been personal because Reagan did have an interesting personal diplomacy, establishing personal connections. Just take one example: In the Japanese case, it worked to some extent. There was a Japanese prime minister, Nakosone, who was prime minister for five years in the mid-1980s, and there was established some kind of personal rapport. So the way the Japanese press saw Reagan was in terms of that personal relationship. This did not always work because Nakosone was not a particularly popular prime minister. So Reagan's popularity may have suffered. The problem was Nakosone's.

The message one got from that was not what I was emphasizing this morning. That is, I think the public image that Reagan imparted to Asian countries was that of a cold warrior, one who was strong and standing quite tough to the communists and the Russians, even making use of China toward and against the Soviet Union. That kind of tough-mindedness, emphasis on military defense, came through. But my sense is that it was a rather false image, a distorted view of what the Reagan presidency was trying to achieve. What the Reagan presidency was trying to achieve was more economically oriented and not trying to solve many of the chronic issues. Apart from his talk about free trade, however, which was quite clear, specifically what kind of vision he had for an Asian economic order, I think, was much less clear.

Philip Khoury. I'm not sure Reagan was the great communicator when it comes to the region of the world I know best, the Middle

East. In fact, I think he was fundamentally uninterested in the Middle East, particularly in the very ugly, difficult issue of the Arabs and Israelis and how to reconcile them. He preferred not to communicate on this subject. He had, however, a number of very close friends from his Hollywood days, who had very strong ties to Israel, and through his relations with them he developed, I think, a much deeper sympathy for Israel than other presidents. Reagan saw Israel as very much worth doing something for. And on a personal level I think he felt very strongly about strengthening the American-Israeli relationship. The difference between Reagan and Carter is that Carter actually tried to engage in statesmanship in the Middle East. He actually brought together the two most important leaders in the region, Sadat and Begin, and forced them to sit in a room at Camp David for fourteen days and hammer out an extremely important accord. It was something that Ronald Reagan could never imagine doing. He never had the attention span necessary for that kind of endeavor. But it's also possible that the opportunities weren't there the way they were earlier. In Reagan's years in office, there was no breakthrough upon which to capitalize, the way Carter had been able to capitalize on Sadat's sudden visit to Jerusalem in 1977.

As for the rest of the Middle East, the Soviets were already occupying Afghanistan by the time Reagan came to power, and in Iran, Khomeini's leadership also was absolutely unfathomable, not only for Ronald Reagan but also for most of his administration.

I think it's a shame that Reagan didn't take a greater positive interest in Middle East peace efforts. The Middle East isn't only important because of its oil. I can't think of a region in the world that's more dangerous for the escalation of superpower competition. We all love to talk about Mr. Gorbachev today and the rosy picture that's being painted of people holding hands in Lenin Square, but one mustn't forget that this is all very recent. And while the Soviet situation is a very promising development, one ought to look more closely at the first six years of Ronald Reagan's presidency, or at least the first term, as I think John Gaddis already pointed out, and remember how tense relations were between the U.S. and the Soviet Union. Relations were particularly tense over the Middle East.

Susanne Jonas. Well, taking off from that, I'll say the opposite, which is that my area of the world would have been a lot better if he had taken less interest rather than more interest. Certainly people in Central America wished that Washington would just forget about it. I've never really gotten into the whole question of Reagan's psyche—what did he really believe and what didn't he believe, and what proportion of the extreme neo-conservatives view he actually believed. I do know that a very high proportion of what he personally said about Central America, and in particular Nicaragua, was false information, just untrue information. His own Drug Enforcement Agency had to correct him when he charged the top Sandinista leaders with running drugs; the DEA issued a statement the next day saying that it was the Contras that were running the drugs, not the Sandinistas. It may be that he didn't know the difference or had forgotten but the proportion of untruth that came out particularly during the years '82 through '86, that is, before Iran-Contra, is absolutely astounding.

The second point is how often it happened. This man got on the radio every Saturday morning and an unbelievable proportion of those Saturday morning addresses were devoted to the question of Central America. Did people buy it? I think the answer is no, because that was a fair amount of presidential energy to pour into a particular subject, yet the public opinion polls never changed (except twice for two weeks each time, once after the invasion of Grenada: for two weeks the opinion ratings of his handling of Central America rose and then they went right back down; the second time after Oliver North testified: there was this same little blip, and then the polls went back down). With these brief exceptions, two-thirds or above of public opinion didn't approve of what Reagan was doing in Central America. They clearly voted for him in 1984 in spite of his Central America policy.

On the last question of what Reagan knew about Contragate: it is a big unknown and I understand from this morning's paper that we may not know, because they quashed the request for

Reagan to appear at the Iran-Contra trial of Oliver North. But there is an open question, only now beginning to come to the fore, of whether he might have known more than we knew that he knew. In any case, I think Central America turned out to be his nemesis.

Robert Rotberg. You all remember that the hedgehog knows one idea well and the fox knows many ideas in different degrees. I think we had a hedgehog as a president. He had a notion on taxes and some notions on other areas. With regard to Africa, he had this profound bias against black Africans—most of the people of Africa—and he was, I think, reinforced by some of his cronies—the kitchen cabinet. I am reminded also of a very telling piece in the *New York Times Magazine* that Les Gelb wrote two years ago, which analyzed Reagan's ideology and indicated that he really learned everything he knew about the world from the movies, from acting in the movies and seeing the movies. This is not really pop psychology. It might actually be close to the truth that he internalized a lot of the roles and the process of thought. With regard to Africa (this is the cheap shot), he may have felt that *Tarzan* was the movie of Africa and reacted that way.

I wondered about that throughout the eight years because his reactions were so simplistic at the crudest possible level. He referred early in the eighties to the present South African rulers as having been staunch allies of the United States and Britain in both world wars. Quickly it was pointed out to him by his own staff that such was the opposite of the truth, that in fact the white leaders of South Africa had mostly been interned because of their pro-Nazi views. It didn't make much difference. He continued to parrot the same ideas, and we the citizenry shrugged it off. He was the great communicator, even if he communicated the wrong ideas. But Africans, not being Americans—not having that marvelous American quality of understanding lots of things happening at once—really resented the notion that he could be so wrong on South Africa. Then he got it wrong on Nigeria, Kenya, and various other places. He got it profoundly the wrong way around, couldn't read the briefing book, didn't really understand, had to be corrected, and had to be reconfigured the next day by his spokesman. That happened so often on the African side of things as well as on taxes and on what happened in the recent American past that one wonders if the hedgehog wasn't really a very programmed hedgehog and that we accomplished, as I said at the very outset of my talk, an enormous amount of reasonable quality in the world despite the presidency and, given the questions you've asked, despite the fact that the rest of the world didn't take it as tolerantly as we did and didn't understand the teflon quality of the presidency the way we did. The American political system is unique. And I mean that in the very best sense. That's not a pejorative comment. And we were able to really shade things in a way which most of the world, particularly the Third World with its zero sum mentality, clearly cannot. For them it sticks. Here nothing sticks.

Geir Lundestad. I've done a fair bit of reading and some research on most presidents starting with Hoover and I think that there can be no doubt that Reagan was clearly the most ignorant of all these presidents. I think there can be little doubt that he was also the laziest of these presidents, but I think it would be entirely wrong to stop there. He was at the same time a political genius.

Look at the hard-working presidents and the presidents who really tried to be informed about everything. I would mention two in particular: Herbert Hoover and Jimmy Carter. History has not been very nice to them. So apparently political success is something different from being well informed, which certainly helps but it's not a crucial ingredient, and it's not the same as hard work, which also helps but it's not a crucial ingredient. Reagan was particularly a genius in that he was able to associate himself with overall American values, make them political in a way, and make them work to his advantage.

When Reagan would speak, he would speak on general topics and notions. He would be all in favor of America. He would be all in favor of optimism, anti-communism, religion, law and order, technology, and hard work even. I think it was part of his stroke of genius that he was able to associate himself and make these typically American values work to his advantage. He was in a way protected by his ignorance and by his laziness. After every press conference, his early press conferences, there would be reports in the *New York Times,* the *Washington Post* and on all the news channels: "Well, these are the fifteen mistakes Reagan made today." This was the tone of the early period. After a while, people didn't care. Even the *Washington Post* and the *New York Times* stopped printing these things. You took it for granted that there would be the correction after his press conference as always. I think part of the explanation for this teflon effect is that he simply operated on a different level. He talked about these values, made them work in his favor, and the Democrats had no idea how they would handle this because they were all in favor of them, too. But that was kind of meek, and yet they couldn't attack it.

I would have certain disagreements with John on how well Reagan planned these things. How well did he know in 1981 where he would be in 1988? It looked pretty bad for Reagan in 1982–83. His foreign policy was generally pretty much of a disaster in that relations became worse with practically everyone, the Soviets, the Europeans. He even had trouble with the Chinese. And the Third World, of course, was his weak spot all the time generally. He combined, he changed, he adjusted course to some extent. And I think this is another part of his secret. He was a very principled politician, very ideological if you want. At least he was perceived as very ideological, but he was also very pragmatic.

It's very difficult to try to combine these two. Being pragmatic you easily undermine your principles. Reagan was actually in a unique way able to combine principle and pragmatism. I've been here for a full year and the last time I was here for an extended stay was in the fall of 1983 when I saw how Reagan handled Lebanon masterfully, just masterfully. He kept talking about the importance of having the troops there as an essential part of his Middle East policy. When there was a dramatic cost to that policy, when these 240-some people got killed, out they went, out they went. Everything was forgotten about all the statements made by Reagan and Shultz about the importance of Beirut and how crucial this element was. Yet he survived this. He combined principles and pragmatism. It was pretty well done.

John Gaddis. It's known as the Aiken strategy. It's what we should have done in Vietnam: declare we won and then leave.

David Kyvig. What Geir has suggested appears to run in a somewhat different direction from your suggestion, John, about the nature of the Reagan record.

John Gaddis. I'm not sure it really does. If you take this concept of negotiation from strength, which I think he took very literally, the implication of that was that you had to build up some strength. That clearly meant that you would not put a high priority on negotiations in the first couple of years until you had restored some sense of self-confidence and until you had built up what almost everybody acknowledged was a military establishment that had been allowed to erode. I don't see it as necessarily inconsistent. What he did say clearly all the way through was that, when you have achieved strength, you should negotiate. That's in the record and I'm inclined to think he meant it fairly literally. I don't think that's necessarily a contradiction.

Geir Lundestad. I think the essential word here is plan. What do we mean when we use the word plan? I think you have to differentiate between long term and short term. Sure there was a long-term plan, which had to do with what John was talking about, negotiating from strength. It has always been a part of American thinking. As Kennan presented this, you would build, you would contain, and then the Soviets would at some stage mellow. So there was this kind of curious combination of pessimism, the threat is very dramatic, but also optimism, in the long run, we're just bound to win. It's very American, we still win. So in that sense, of course, there had always been the containment "plan."

But in a short-term perspective, I think it's unlikely that Reagan had any kind of detailed plan because if you look at the phrases he used, it seems to me that they do not indicate an expectation of short-term results. If you talk about "cheat and lie" and "evil empire," than you don't really expect results tomorrow. You expect results sometime in the future. So I think the process went considerably quicker than Reagan had thought in 1982–83. I agree with John certainly that the charges were underway well before Gorbachev and well before the 1984 election. But the element of Reagan having a plan in a more concrete, short-term sense, I think that's something else.

John Gaddis. There's a difference between plans and instincts. He may not have had good plans, but he had good instincts. He had the same instincts as a good poker player. You do a certain amount of bluffing, you know when to hold and when to fold. That sort of thing.

Robert Rotberg. John, you can't support that from the Reykjavik negotiations where he blew it, upset his allies, worried the NSC, and when he gave away everything because he wasn't sufficiently well briefed. I think Geir made a very good point that Presidents Eisenhower and Reagan were very popular and did as little as possible and knew as little as possible and the most knowledgeable or the brightest president we've ever had, Carter, was too bright. That's a terrible thing to say in a university setting. And it is terrible, too, what Geir said about the barbarian instincts of Americans will now go down the drain as a result of your conclusions.

John Gaddis. But you're not allowing for Eisenhower revisionism.

Robert Rotberg. Not enough, no. I worked in the executive office building during his presidency and I have some personal views which are different from Fred Greenstein's and others. And I think that you'd have to look at it case by case to see whether Reagan's instincts were right. I would say that his instincts were disastrously wrong domestically. And if we look internationally, I can't see where those instincts are right except, and here's where I agree with what's just been said, he could say we will win and then take the credit for a realignment in the Soviet Union. But I would argue that we are the beneficiaries of something over which we had very little control, some influence, but very little control.

Susanne Jonas. I think that the changes in the Soviet Union were completely unpredictable; Washington didn't have a very clear understanding of what was happening. But beyond that, different things were going on in different parts of the world. On the basis of having spent twenty-two years looking at Latin America, I can say that U.S. policymakers don't understand very much of the dynamics of those societies. No matter what is actually going on, they impose a geopolitical perspective which blinds them. I began my talk today pointing out that in Central America one assumes they know what is going on because they have four allies in the region. They've been able to control these four allies up until now and they assume that's the way it's going to go. And all of a sudden in 1987 there were five Central American presidents saying no to the Contra policy. To a very profound degree that came from the fact that they—not just Reagan, but U.S. policymakers since the Kennedy administration—have faced the same problems vis-a-vis Latin America. There are changes that take place there that they never understand, either because they don't want to, or because they can't—they continually recast reality with a geopolitical overlay, explaining everything in Central America in terms of the Soviet Union and U.S.-Soviet geopolitical relations. The press does this, too, including very, very respectable leading journalists. But I think they hadn't been down there and so there were many things they didn't quite understand about why these changes occurred in the region. Perhaps this is true for other parts of the Third World, too. But I do have a very strong feeling that in the case of Latin America at least, they still don't quite have a clue. These austerity riots in Venezuela are just the most recent example. Venezuela is their model; it's everybody's model of the way Latin America should go except that they have just killed 300 people in riots because of the debt problem. And I think that's a symbol for many other things.

John Gaddis. I would have assumed, Susanne, exactly what you say: They don't have a clue when it comes to these regions. I think that's not only characteristic of Reagan, but it's been characteristic of most postwar administrations when you get into Third World areas. Lyndon Johnson didn't know much about Southeast Asia either. The difference between Lyndon Johnson and Ronald Reagan was that Johnson within a year and half of taking office had committed something like 150,000 troops in Southeast Asia. Reagan committed fifty-five to El Salvador and trained some in Honduras, but that was it. How many times did Ortega predict the imminent American invasion of Nicaragua that never did come off? What I'm talking about here is not sophisticated knowledge of the Third World; what I'm talking about is a sense of political reality with regard to the United States and what the American people over the long haul are prepared to support. And I would argue that on this score Ronald Reagan was far more perceptive than Lyndon Johnson.

Susanne Jonas. He also had Johnson's tremendous error to learn from.

John Gaddis. One always hopes that one will learn from history, but don't count on it.

David Kyvig. One of the themes running through this discussion seems to be comprehension and planning in the Reagan foreign policy. And I'm wondering what those we haven't yet heard from on this question perceive as the level of comprehension of Reagan and his inner circle about the peculiar circumstances of their regions of the world. Also, how coherent was Reagan policy from January 1981 to January 1989? Do we see evidence of planning, or do we see signs of luck and misfortune, but not a coherent approach?

Akira Iriye. I would say that vis-a-vis East Asia he may have been somewhat knowledgeable or may have taken a more personal interest. I think being from California may have made some difference in that he is Pacific-oriented. He keeps talking about the Pacific century or the Pacific age. And I think he was among the first leaders to notice and publicly state the fact that in 1984 American trade in the Pacific exceeded American trade with Europe. He made a big thing out of it as indicative of the fact that American economic interests may be turning westward to Asia. I think having lived half his life in California may have given rise to that Pacific orientation. It was rather flattering, obviously, to the people in Asia that he was a president who was fairly knowledgeable about Asia, who was interested in their affairs, certainly far more so than others. Even though Lyndon Johnson knew something about Asia, that didn't quite work out, as John was saying, to America's advantage.

Another thing one could say for Reagan's presidency is that he had some very good advisors and ambassadors. Mike Mansfield as Reagan's ambassador to Japan was a spectacular success. There's no question about it. He understood the country. He was a very constructive force, I think, in mitigating some of the irritants in U.S.-Japanese relations. Reagan did have some instincts about putting the right people in the right areas. I think Winston Lord in Beijing was another good choice as U.S. ambassador. Richard Armacost, who is now going to be ambassador to Japan, was ambassador to the Philippines and later on returned to Washington as undersecretary of state for East Asian affairs. As far as I can tell, he was quite knowledgeable. He was an Asian major in undergraduate days, and he once taught school in Japan. So he has some very good knowledge about that part of the world. And it seems to me that Reagan may have had the right people in the right spots during the Philippine crisis a few years ago. The decision to abandon Marcos and support Aquino, I think, was a good choice. And it did reflect the information he or his aides had. So on balance I have to say that things could have been much worse. There are some bright spots in Asia.

Philip Khoury. I can't say the same for one good reason. People who have followed the National Security Council over the years tell me that there has never been a more uniformly inexperienced staff than during Reagan's presidency. Certainly it was in evidence most recently with the Iran-Contra fiasco. From the beginning of his administration, Middle East experts were very frightened by his appointments, about who was making decisions, and about who was whispering in the president's ear. The level of incompetence was really quite remarkable. The Middle East conflicts have nothing to do with sympathy; they require understanding and comprehension, something the NSC staff failed to achieve for eight years.

If you look at Arabs and Israelis and their conflict of forty-plus years, the Arabs have been spoiled by aggressive presidents who desired a strong interventionist policy in the Middle East.

And I include Henry Kissinger in that pantheon of presidents. When Nixon was hobbled by the Watergate scandal, Kissinger ran foreign policy all by himself, and he was very skillful. I didn't like everything he did, but he knew how to leave a positive impression on the Arab leaders, something Carter also did. Even the president of Syria, whom we have a lot of trouble with, Hafiz al-Asad, had to appreciate the fact that Henry Kissinger knocked on his door regularly, trying to work out the disengagement accords of 1974–75. This was extremely important to the Arab leaders who have a lot of difficulties and divisions but who unanimously concur that the United States government has not been even-handed vis-a-vis the Arabs and Israelis.

As far as the Israeli's are concerned, they want an American president who will stand up and say "we're behind you," but then who will back off and not tell them how to run their own affairs. And Ronald Reagan was very much that kind of president. He created the strategic alliance. He and his advisers worked this out. As a result, the Israeli-American relationship has never been stronger, never more secure. But, I believe that in spite of this strategic alliance, if Washington doesn't persuade Israel to bend a bit, to moderate some of her commitment to the continued occupation of the West Bank and Gaza, this will not redound to Israel's long-term benefit. In the end, the U.S. may lose its influence with the moderate wing in the Arab world, which may not have a great deal of clout today, but which one day may turn things around. In this regard, I think Ronald Reagan hasn't been very helpful.

But I have a lot of trouble concentrating on Ronald Reagan, because he wasn't actively interested, let alone well informed, about the various Middle East conflicts. Rather, we ought to be looking at who was around Ronald Reagan. Foreign policy is not a one-man show in a democracy. He was getting advice from different elements in his administration, from an administration, incidentally, whose turnover of ranking personnel was higher than in any previous administration. Think of the officials who started with Ronald Reagan and think of who was left at the end. One has to keep in mind the high turnover rate. Why haven't we focused our discussion on the so-called experts or the technicians or the people who might actually have plans and designs and be trying to get their president to approve them, or who go ahead and implement them without approval?

In the case of the Middle East, I can't say that the Reagan advisers produced a great plan or scheme or strategy. There was an attempt to try to lure Iran back and that wasn't an entirely bad idea. If one could moderate Iran somehow, one could then bring a very ugly conflict to an end, and thereby strengthen America's hand in the region. So the idea of trying to work with Iran I don't think was a bad thing. But the methods that were employed were outrageous, outlandish. The Reagan administration insulted the American people with its devious maneuvers at a time when the Iranians were supporting the continued holding of American hostages in Lebanon, when they were blowing up various American institutions, when they were basically a destabilizing force. So, as far as the Middle East is concerned, maybe we ought to ignore Ronald Reagan for a moment and look at who was in his administration and what goes on at State and what goes on at the NSC and how do the intelligence agencies play their roles. Was there any kind of unified strategy in the various Third World areas or vis-a-vis Europe and Russia? I don't know. John Gaddis seems to think that this was the case for Russia. History may prove John right; John's argument is very powerful but not completely convincing. In other areas of the world, the Third World in particular, American policy under Reagan seems less well thought out or successful than it was for Russia or Japan.

David Kyvig. I would like to intervene at this point and invite people from the audience to ask questions.

*Jane Leonard.** I would like to come back to Philip Khoury's point here and to a question about the institutions and the agencies of foreign policy. I am reminded that back in 1969 Edmund Clubb gave a very interesting talk at the Asian Studies meeting called "The Effect of the McCarthy Period on Field Reporting of Asian Affairs." Essentially what he was saying was that the politics of the national security state are such that the top level of the administration no longer listens or seeks to find plans from

*Asterisked participants are Professors of History at the University of Akron.

the experts in State or the field officers. Careerism plays a much more important role in formulation of foreign policies. So I would like to know in the various areas that all these experts represent what agencies and what sort of dynamics within the government have been most influential in directing or driving foreign relations initiatives.

John Gaddis. Somebody asked yesterday about the role of the State Department, and I made the argument that as far as Soviet-American relations were concerned, the department was fairly important in the second part of the administration, particularly after George Shultz became secretary of state. I think what happened in relations with the Soviet Union was probably quite consistent with what the professional Soviet experts in the State Department thought should happen, with one or two exceptions. Bob Rotberg mentioned Rekjavik a while ago. Of course, Rekjavik is entirely a special case on both sides and still quite inexplicable. But allowing for the general drift of policy, I think it's probably fair to say that it came out pretty close to what State wanted.

Akira Iriye. I think it's a very interesting picture depending on which area of Asia you look at. Regarding Japan, I would say the most important agency of the government is not the State Department, not the National Security Council, not even the White House, but the so-called U.S.T.R., United States Trade Representative, because of the importance of the trade question. It has been extremely important and that has been the problem, because it's not very well supported by the president and by Congress. It's not very well understood, I guess, by the people. So it's understaffed. I think the number of staff that concentrates on Asian affairs is less than ten. There are a handful of people working day and night on these trade issues, trade disputes with Japan. It's very competent. I know some of the people who are on the U.S.T.R. They are as knowledgeable as you would hope to get. But they are all overworked. But it does seem to me that regarding trade issues, that's where you'd go.

For China one turns naturally to things like security, of course, because of Reagan's emphasis on security issues regarding China. The Pentagon and the National Security Council play more important roles than the State Department. In a case like the Philippines' transition from Marcos to Aquino, something like the U.S.I.A., United States Information Agency, may have played as important a role as any because of the need for precise information. Who's going to turn out to vote? Marcos is engaged in his own propaganda campaign saying that Aquino had no future, which turned out to be wrong. From what I gather, there was accurate information coming out from U.S.I.A. offices in the Philippines from the village level that there was a strong swell of opposition to Marcos and, therefore, that the United States should not stand in the way of Aquino's victory. And Reagan's decision not to do that but in fact to recognize Aquino I think was the correct decision and may have been based on these reports coming from the U.S.I.A.

So I think there are different agencies involved. The State Department does not play the role it used to as the only agency in charge of foreign affairs. Regarding Edmund Clubb's talk about the decimation of China experts during the McCarthy era, I think that was terribly serious. We all know that. But my impression is that because of the National Defense Education Act and various other government-sponsored programs in the '60s and '70s, there have emerged a new generation of China experts and Asian experts who know the language, who know the culture, and so on. My sense is that the junior officers who are middle-ranking officers in the State Department and A.I.D. and U.S.I.A. are very qualified people. Those that I have met seem to be as good as the China hands who were there first.

Philip Khoury. In the case of the Middle East at least, under Reagan the experts are located, and historically they've been located in the State Department. They are known, and this should define their reputation instantly, as the "Arabists." When we're dealing with the Arab-Israeli conflict being identified as an Arabist doesn't necessarily mean the experts are pro-Arab, but that's what their detractors really mean. The Arabists have basically been pushing paper for the better part of forty years, but to no avail.

When there is a strong secretary of state who knows what he is doing, such as Henry Kissinger, one can count on a very active State Department, but only at the highest echelons. Not necessarily, however, in the long term doing things that bring peace and justice to the Middle East; but they're at least trying to stabilize and manage a very serious conflict. And Kissinger had considerable success in doing so after the October 1973 war. On the other hand, if one thinks of William Rogers and his peace plans, or Cyrus Vance and his plans, they ended up in the wastebasket. Either the National Security Council persuaded the president that these plans were unworkable or members of Congress let the president know, or let their friends at the National Security Council know, that what State was up to was something that was unhealthy for domestic reasons. Over the years the State Department experts have been what I would call "even-handed." They think first and foremost of U.S. interests and that's what they are supposed to do. U.S. interests require greater even-handedness in the Arab-Israeli conflict if there is to be some kind of settlement and stabilization of that conflict. That hasn't happened in the Reagan administration years. I think George Shultz will not be written down as an effective secretary of state owing to his Middle East policies. In fact, I can't think of a secretary of state who has been less effective than Shultz. But, only time will prove me right or wrong.

One ought to look at the Defense Department when one talks about the Middle East. And here it's quite interesting to note that Casper Weinberger ended up identified with the Arabist crowd. He was considered too even-handed and therefore many of his efforts to keep administration policy balanced on the Arab-Israeli conflict and even vis-a-vis Iran and Iraq in their war were criticized by the NSC staff.

And I think it's very important when one thinks about foreign policy in the Middle East to think about the role of the U.S. Congress. Congress doesn't initiate policy, but it has a remarkable amount of influence when it comes to how arms are going to be traded, what sort of treaties are going to be signed, what's going to be sold, and so on. And in the case of the Middle East, we have a very active Congress. Perhaps more active than on any other region I can think of, at least as far as the Third World is concerned, even more so perhaps than Latin America, which I find rather remarkable given that Latin America is our back-

yard. But then the stakes are much higher in the Middle East
because of oil and strategic considerations, the level of conflict
has been that much higher as well. Here, one can't ignore
the strong influences that domestic lobbies and constituencies
have exercised over Congress and its attitudes toward the Middle
East.

Susanne Jonas. I'd like to separate it out into two different levels. There is an operative consensus about Latin America in terms
of keeping the hemisphere free of communism, etc. And then
there's the particular overlay given to policy under the Reagan
administration, which led them to try to overthrow the Nicaraguan government. In terms of understanding where did the policy in general come from, there probably is a fairly stable con-
glomeration of influences. And actually I'd broaden what Phil
started to say, which is to look at the groups like the Council on
Foreign Relations where the corporate foreign policy thinkers do
their thinking. Their opinions do come into play and keep a certain kind of balance or concensus about policy. They never stop
thinking that if there's an insurgency in Latin America you have
to intervene to put it down. This is what I referred to this morning as the bipartisan consensus and the remarkable, absolutely
remarkable absence of any debate about El Salvador. At some
point they may find themselves in a position where they intervene openly or let it go. But up until now, as long as they think
they don't have to make that choice, there's really no debate
over policy whatsoever. This has been operative since the '60s—
including that some of the same people have been involved since
then (for example, in the Defense Department). These people
are absolutely essential in terms of keeping a certain kind of
direction to what we're going to do in Latin America, not just
Central America. That's one sort of norm.

Now add to that the rise of a particular ideological current,
the New Right, the neo-conservatives, which Reagan began to
articulate and which was reflected in the 1980 Republican party
platform: We're going after the Sandinista government in Nicaragua. We're not going to let it stand. That was the novelty of
the Reagan policy—roll back.

So I think you just have to look at these different levels in terms of trying to explain institutionally where these things come from. It is likely that the Reagan years have changed the picture permanently. I don't think that just because the New Right is out of the driver's seat right now, their influence will totally subside. Their ideas have shifted everybody's ideas to some extent, and I think it'll take a long time and maybe another big disaster before that will change. One example is the document *Discriminate Deterrence,* which is authored by people who are from that New Right current but has the support of people like Brzezinski and Kissinger. It is basically an argument that now that the Cold War is winding down with the Soviet Union, we can pull back some from Europe, but the Third World will require much more security assistance with less restrictions. These ideas are written down there in black and white in their report and I haven't heard very much argument or debate about it. So I think in terms of putting Reagan into historical perspective, we have to look at what was "abnormal" and then go back to what are the constants of U.S. policy regardless of particular administrations.

And finally just in terms of the Elliott Abrams phenomenon: Abrams was no Latin Americanist. None of us Latin Americanists had ever heard of Elliott Abrams before. He just wasn't a particularly knowledgeable person. He was somebody who came out of the ranks of that group on the New Right. And the person they're putting in as his successor, Bernard Aronson, shares many of his ideas. That suggests that neo-conservatives view Central America as a little preserve where they're going to continue to exercise a great deal of influence. So I don't think we've seen the last of this particular set of debates.

Robert Rotberg. If one were a professional foreign service officer, one would want to be ambassador to a relatively small out-of-the-way country, because then one could really have a kind of influence locally that ambassadors no longer have. Being ambassador to France is relatively boring. There's very little one can do; one gets instructions by cable. One reports back and gets further instructions. Whereas in Burundi, or in Malawi, ambassadors can have a major impact. In Africa, given a White House that wasn't terribly concerned about anything except winning or losing the global struggle, if Chester Crocker could persuade the White House that that's what he was doing, then he could essentially do what he wanted. That's a reasonable way to look at Africa, which is not of central strategic importance to the United States. At a second level, given poverty, famine, overpopulation, and so on, it is of greater strategic importance, but that's not where the Reagan administration was coming from. And, therefore, Crocker did have a great deal of room to organize African policy. But Crocker, even though an academic, was a political appointment. He was Bush's Africa person, which is how he got the job originally. And the distinction that I would like to make is again something that is a throwback to Kissinger. You can have all the knowledge in the world, and there is a great deal of knowledge in the third, fourth, and fifth floors of the State Department, but it wasn't percolating to the sixth and seventh floors. And probably still isn't.

The enormous amount of work done—good work done in the lower levels of the State Department or in the field—never was allowed to impact upon policy. If you take the one big area, South Africa, you see policy being made by Crocker and his chief aides, two or three people, on the basis of the same kind of seat of the pants analytical ability that Kissinger had. That is, wanting an objective, finding a way to do it, going forward, sending instructions out, not really listening even to a political appointee in South Africa, and not really taking the inputs from there. If you take Nigeria, half the population of black Africa, no attention was paid to the repository of information in the field. Africa's a peculiar place, too, because other than in a few troubled areas, the station chiefs, the CIA people in Africa, have relatively little impact. In the Angolan war, we relied on British intelligence for much of our knowledge. Our intercept capability wasn't very great.

The Department of Defense didn't impact terribly much. The Department of Defense and the National Security Agency were both to the left of the State Department, which is an incredible thing to say, on most issues in Africa. They understood how unimportant Africa was to a lot of strategic considerations, which Crocker and the State Department didn't. So it can get very complicated, but in a short answer, Africa was a special place and Crocker had it all to himself and ignored the State Department just as thoroughly as Kissinger did during his time and as did the rest of the State Department.

Geir Lundestad. The principals decide what they want to decide. So when the assistant secretaries have a lot of freedom to maneuver that is a reflection, as Bob suggested, either of support or the lack of interest on the part of the principals. I think in Western Europe it was, certainly after the pipeline dispute had been resolved, a very orderly process in the sense that the president was reasonably interested in what was going on. The State Department worked fairly well. The secretary of state was interested. The assistant secretary, Roseanne Ridgeway, was very knowledgeable about European affairs and had the confidence of most Europeans. The Pentagon, of course, was somewhat special and somewhat at odds with the State Department. There was Weinberger and there was Richard Perle, of course, but then we get into arms control issues, which became an important part of American-European relations as well.

The one important element I would like stress is the input of the Europeans, which became considerable, particularly after the pipeline dispute had been resolved. Of course, Margaret Thatcher played a very important role. She played an important role in not only the Falklands issue and Libya, but she was instrumental in redefining to some extent the nature of SDI, making it more compatible to European interests, making it part of a negotiating strategy. And she was very instrumental in redefining the American posture after Reykjavik. Of course, in Europe and Britain the left generally tend to think of Thatcher being dominated by Reagan. I think she held her own pretty much in that relationship. She knew what she wanted, and she was ready to speak up at any time. From what we know about these meetings, she was very forceful. And the president listened. There was also input from other European countries.

When the principals take such an interest, then, of course, the influence of others will be reduced. I think Europe is not really comparable to East Asia in the sense that the ambassadors had such an important role. Some of the U.S. ambassadors to Europe were disappointments. I think of the American ambassador to France. He was not a very knowledgeable person. He did not have a lot of influence either.

James Richardson.* We in the Ohio Academy of History heard Michael Hogan talk last fall about his investigation of two periods of Anglo-American relationships. In the 1920s he saw the president's hands all over the place. The president had very direct involvement, and he was heavily influential in the design of policy. In the 1940s, Hogan said he may have had two references to Truman in his index. In a sense the institutional structure of American foreign policy or national security became so fully developed that the president was a less important actor after World War II than prior to that time. Do you think it might happen, if we would hold a conference like this twenty years from now, that we would be talking much more about things like NSC and various other groups and making only minimal reference to Ronald Reagan?

John Gaddis. I don't know that I agree with that. I know what Mike Hogan is talking about. Truman himself was not that personally engaged in the making of policy. The same would not have been true of Eisenhower. Eisenhower would have had his footprints all over the place, based on the archival evidence that we have now. Certainly the same would have been true of Kennedy and LBJ, and Nixon, too, I expect. What you have with Truman is simply the fact that, although we think of him as an activist president, in foreign policy he very much left things up to his subordinates. But he did a good job choosing subordinates. I wouldn't project that pattern forward and generalize from that about all successive presidents.

Sheldon Liss.* I'd like to follow up on something that you talked about previously pertaining to the people who were making the decisions during the Reagan administration. For fifteen years prior to the Reagan administration, those of us in the field of U.S.-Latin American relations would periodically get calls from Washington. We would be asked to go to Washington. Our opin-

ion would be solicited and then generally nobody paid any attention to us. In the first year of the Reagan administration, the
assistant secretary of state made it very clear to me, and I'll
quote from him directly, "We don't give a shit what you people
think. We're going to do what we're going to do." Then they
proceeded to appoint almost the entire Vietnam team to Latin
America. They put people into positions and into embassies
throughout Latin America who had formerly served in the embassy and various underling positions in South Vietnam. And
the same exact thing happened, of course, with Elliott Abrams.
Elliott Abrams knew nothing about Latin America, spoke not
one word of Spanish, and had never been in the area. Yet the
very week after he was appointed to that position, I saw him in
Washington, D.C., giving the State Department's position on Latin
American affairs. It was very clear that it was an ideology that
they were interested in perpetuating, that they didn't look for
expertise, that they didn't want expertise. Incidentally, for the
balance of the Reagan administration, probably 90 percent of the
people in the academic world who are specialists in U.S.-Latin
American relations, with many of them being conservatives, were
not ever called upon to testify. And the most reactionary, not
even conservative but most reactionary people in the field, most
of whom were failed academics who couldn't cut it in various
universities, including people like Mark Falcoff who Susanne
mentioned before, were brought to Washington, D.C., and worked
with the American Enterprise Institute, the Heritage Foundation, and so forth. These were the people who were feeding ideas
into the people who were working in the various Central American desks.

Philip Khoury. Let me compare and contrast what you pointed
out for Latin America with the case of the Middle East. The
assistant secretary of state for Near Eastern affairs was Richard
Murphy. Murphy is a trained Arabist, a former ambassador to
Damascus, a very competent individual. I would put him maybe
a rung below Harold Saunders who was assistant secretary of
state in the Carter administration. In fact, Murphy knew much
more about the Middle East than Saunders did. He just wasn't

as good at pushing paper around and getting it up to the sixth or seventh floor at state. But in Murphy's case, he had to deal with a secretary of state who would not listen to him and was really not paying a great deal of attention to the Middle East, particularly after the Lebanon fiasco of 1983–84. Basically Shultz turned his back on the Middle East until the Palestinian uprising in late 1987, which forced him to get back into it. Again, I return to the idea that if you don't have a receptive secretary of state who's going to carry your ideas forward or at least wrestle with them a bit and then think of carrying them forward, you're in trouble. So an expert like Murphy who was, I think, a very thoughtful, balanced, intelligent individual got absolutely nowhere. Murphy faced six years of total frustration in trying to move policy forward.

Susanne Jonas. On the Latin American score, I think it's a mixed bag. I want to come back to the two levels I mentioned before. Very likely they picked Abrams for his bully qualities as much as anything else, for his ability to stand up to everyone. Who knows why they particularly picked him or whom he knew, or why he got that job. First, I think it is significant that his successor is someone with such similar views. Secondly, it's important to understand that there was some continuity in the State Department with some of the Latin American experts from Carter to Reagan. Not all of them quit; some of them just made their adjustment. Luigi Einaudi stands out in my mind as an example. He was a Rand person who went to the State Department first, I believe, under Carter, and when Reagan came in just stayed there and switched lines. He is extremely knowledgeable; I don't agree with him on anything, but the man is extremely well informed. So I don't think it's simply a question of ignorance. I think there are a number of different things going on. There probably are points at which knowledgeable people can put in their expertise, but then their knowledge is used to prove whatever it is that they wanted to prove to begin with. If someone like Einaudi had not proven willing to make that switch to the Reagan line himself, he probably wouldn't have lasted. They'll use the Latin American experts when they prove usable and when they don't, they won't. And I don't think any administration, by

the way, would ever listen to 90 percent of the Latin Americanists in this country because if there is a particularity of Latin
American studies, it's that most people who begin to study Latin
America are appalled by what they find about the relationship
between the United States and Latin America. The Latin American Studies Association has a fairly leftist bias, which would
not be acceptable to a Carter administration, a Truman administration, a Kennedy administration, or any other. We'll have to
see what kind of administration would ever take on the LASA
establishment.

In any case, I think "policy expertise" is a mixed bag and not
just one thing: The U.S. government does have its people who
have been there with a fair amount of continuity, who are listened to, and who are not totally unknowledgeable. They just
have a particular view of Latin American reality. One other point:
It's not that they don't have the knowledge about Latin America, they do. I mean they have the entire CIA at their disposal.
So lack of intelligence is not the problem. I think the problem is
sort of the way in which the information is turned to fit a predetermined scheme, to tell them what they want to know to begin with. We need to study their processing of knowledge—what
happens between the time it's reported and when it is used. And
then, generally speaking, the people who don't like what's done
with their knowledge end up resigning and speaking out.

Sheldon Liss. I think it's also sad that some very fine foreign
service officers such as Wayne Smith, head of the U.S. interest
section in Cuba, and Rob White, the ambassador to El Salvador,
who did transcend the administrations, found it necessary to re-
sign from the foreign service a few months into the Reagan administration.

Geir Lundestad. I've been living in Washington this academic
year, and this is, of course, the kind of talk you hear all the time
about the players: who is sitting where and doing what and moving what paper to whom and all this. Of course, this is important. But at the same time I can't refrain from thinking this only
becomes interesting when you take certain other things for
granted. For instance, the fact that even a very passive president is bound to exert tremendous influence in many ways,

starting with the appointments made. These people we're talking about, they're not there by coincidence. They're there because they fit within some sort of wider framework, ideological or otherwise. Thousands of people are moved out when you change administrations and the newcomers, all the players we are talking about, they're there because they have some sort of relationship to the incoming administration. Even a very passive president will set the tone and will, of course, affect who will be brought in. And even a very passive president will have to sign on ultimately to most important decisions. So even if the president does not decide on a course entirely different from what is recommended from below, he sets the tone. I think this can easily be neglected and not paid sufficient attention to by all the people inside the system because they take all of this for granted. I think it's important and should be stated quite clearly.

I would like to bring in another perspective though as a kind of extension of this because we are talking about foreign policy. If you take this kind of reasoning too far, you're making foreign policy sound almost like domestic policy. Foreign policy is, by definition, policy toward at least one other country. And if this policy is to be successful, there are certain criteria that have to be fulfilled. First you have to know what you want. Then there will be the reaction and the input from the other side. I think this should be stressed time and again. The United States and the Soviet Union will achieve very little if they work against the local forces. With the kind of technology you see now, the kind of developments you see now, a few terrorists in Lebanon can kick the U.S. out. That's an extreme example, but it points to the importance of sufficient attention being paid to what is going on in other parts of the world and what the other players are doing. The local scene is tremendously important. In Guatemala it was sufficient to put in 150 men to overthrow the government in 1954. In Nicaragua, thousands can't do it. Why? Well, because, among other things, the local situation is entirely different. Guatemala 1954 could not be repeated in Cuba and could not be repeated in Nicaragua. Why? Because of the local forces. As a foreigner, I almost feel it's my responsibility to insist on the importance of what is going on outside the U.S.

Akira Iriye. I couldn't agree more with that emphasis on the local scene. The question is how do we find out what is going on at the local scene? In reality it is individuals who do the finding and transmitting of information. We come back to the question of the quality of individuals, reporters, intelligence analysts.

Bob Rotberg this morning was mentioning the Peace Corps. I think that kind of thing ought to be taken into consideration, not just the president or ambassadors but what he referred to as people-to-people diplomacy. USIA is important, I think. The Peace Corps is important. I think Rotberg made a very good comment that despite everything else the Reagan administration did maintain the Peace Corps. In fact, I think he increased the size of it. Despite all the budget cutting that he did, trying to create a smaller government, I think one area he did not touch, and in fact he allocated more money, was the USIA, the public diplomacy section. And also the Fulbright program was expanded, which I think is a very good thing because it does indicate the awareness of this kind of contact, profound contact, extensive contact with foreign countries and foreign cultures.

Coming back to the bureaucracy, because I'm the optimist on this panel, I'd also like to say that because of the people in the State Department manning Asian desks, the Japan desk, the China desk, and so on, the lowest rung if we were ranking bureaucrats, is not bad at all. During the 1960s and 70s and 80s when it was very hard to get academic jobs, many people went to Washington to work. And that may have had a very good spillover effect on the quality of the American bureaucracy. I know, from my university, the University of Chicago, three of my top students ended up in the State Department. I think it's good to have these people, these Ph.D.s. One became a China hand. He did not start out that way, but of necessity because he was stationed in China, he got fluency in Chinese and he's there. He works on China policy in the State Department. And whether the president knows that he's there or not is beside the point. It's not as important as the fact that he's there. When the need arises, he can be sent to China for field reporting and so on. I think that kind of thing is what I had in mind when I talked about some degree of confidence about the nature of bureaucracy in the United States.

*J. Wayne Baker.** I wanted to ask Susanne to say something
about Panama and our reaction to recent events there.

Susanne Jonas. Well, in a way it bears out what I was just saying. I'll go back a year to when things first came out. Noriega
was indicted and so on, and the U.S. first began the movement
to get rid of him. People were asking me the very next day,
what's going to happen in Panama? I said I wasn't sure yet. I'll
have to watch this a little bit because I haven't been following it
that closely. This is something that has just come to public attention. And about a week or two later, it became clear that the
U.S. was supporting Delvalle to become the new president. They
had a whole strategy worked out where he was going to be ac-
claimed as president. Now Noriega was, of course, extremely
unpopular, a little dictator in many ways. He is repressive, he's
corrupt. But the day that Delvalle got the tap on the shoulder
from Elliott Abrams, I knew what was going to happen. Obviously Noriega's going to be in there for the long range because
in a situation like that, all that Noriega needed was for Elliott
Abrams to make a move in the direction of his opponent. That
secured him. And he was going to stay—and he's still there.
This bears out how the U.S. often operates blindly, even in terms
of its own logic and its own goals. That wasn't always the case—
sometimes they achieved their goals. But Panama was a real disaster because they did not understand things that happened there
over twenty years ago (like the flag riots of 1964). Any time the
United States comes in there and says here's our man, that person is finished. Some of the structural constraints operating on
U.S. policy right now are not always fully understood in Washington. There are dynamics in these countries, political situations, that really are quite outside the control of the United States.
The more we come in there and try to dictate what's going to
happen, the more likely at this particular moment in history
they're not going to happen that way. So I think that it was
pretty predictable that as soon as we got involved in a big way
in Panama, we would lose control. It's very interesting that the
other people who said precisely the same thing that I'm saying
right now were the people from the U.S. Southern Command.
The more Elliott Abrams started talking about sending in U.S.

forces, the more they said, "Hey wait a minute, we've had this operation going here for many years. You're not going to come in here and mess it all up." The Joint Chiefs of Staff, the Pentagon and the Southern Command wanted to keep the status quo. They're much closer to the ground than a lot of other policy-makers. Not all, but many of them are very pragmatic. The head of the Southern Command now has been down in Central America for twenty-something years; he's been involved in counter-insurgency in Central America, and he certainly does understand many of the dynamics of what's going on. So they told Washington to forget it: Don't talk about U.S. intervention any more, so that we don't get any more of our people stoned or killed or have to move the base tomorrow. So I think Panama was a policy mess; anyone who has studied Panamanian history for the last fifteen years would have had some understanding of the level of nationalism there and could have predicted that Noriega would stay in power once the U.S. determined that he was going to go.

David Kyvig. We have come almost to the end of a two-day conference on the foreign relations of the Reagan administration with only brief mention of Lieutenant Colonel Oliver North. That is remarkable in itself. When Oliver North became a household word, there was a great deal of discussion that what he represented in the largest sense was a fundamental shift in the constitutional arrangements for the conduct of American foreign policy: the balance of authority and responsibility between the executive and Congress, and the extent of presidential power. Was there such a shift during the Reagan years?

John Gaddis. The passage of time already suggests that there was no fundamental shift in the constitutional arrangements for conducting foreign policy during the Reagan administration. Colonel North, it now appears, was a hyperactive functionary who briefly exceeded—or was allowed to exceed—his authority.

Geir Lundestad. Reagan was a popular president and that popularity, of course, strengthened his position vis-a-vis Congress in the constant power struggle between the executive and legislative branches. But on many specific issues Reagan was out of step with popular opinion and that gave Congress the courage to stand up to him on certain specific occasions. The whole issue of the size of the defense budget shows the great importance both of presidential-congressional rivalry and, ultimately, the prevailing role of public opinion. In his first years Reagan was able to get tremendous increases in defense spending; in his second term he got practically nothing. I also think Congress and public opinion helped move Reagan from almost exclusive emphasis on "strength" in the early years to the combination of "peace" and "strength." Congress had a dramatic impact on certain aspects of Reagan's arms control policy and on South Africa.

Reagan was really flexible on most foreign policy issues and that made it easier for him to work with Congress. The two issues where he was really rigid were the Contras and SDI. On SDI he won at least a partial victory over Congress. On the Contras he lost, despite North's transgressions beyond the law.

Philip Khoury. I mentioned Oliver North in my formal presentation and discussed the domestic impact of Iran-Contra on the Reagan administration and its policy in the Middle East. I can't recall a more outrageous and foolish set of covert American activities abroad than those associated with Iran-Contra. The closest parallel is with Watergate, a domestic fiasco, but even Watergate pales by comparison. On the surface, it would seem that North symbolized a shift in the constitutional arrangements for the conduct of American foreign policy. The Constitution clearly is something he and his colleagues had little respect for; they saw it as an obstacle to the achievement of Reagan administration policy aims and therefore they abused it in the pursuit of those aims. That a significant minority of Americans admired North and labeled him a hero suggests that all too many Americans are either ignorant of or have inadequate respect for the Constitution. This doesn't bode well for our democracy.

I'm afraid that kind of abuse that many of us now associate with the Iran-Contra affair is probably nothing more than an extreme variety of what has taken place all too often in the conduct of American foreign policy, particularly in the Third World. One need only think of Central America. Therefore, Iran-Contra was not an aberration nor does it really mark a significant shift in the conduct of American foreign policy. The question remains: will the Iran-Contra revelations produce a meaningful and substantial corrective? I'm not too optimistic given that the major challenges to the conduct of American policy abroad in the next decade are likely to come not from the Soviet Union but from Third World countries that are seeking to assert their independence of both American and Soviet influence.

U.S. Foreign Relations in the Reagan Era: An Early Bibliographic Survey

Books dealing with the foreign policies, performance, and personnel of the Reagan administration appeared with some regularity during its eight years in office. These works, most of them by journalists or former members of the administration, are helpful in constructing a picture of the administration as seen by contemporaries within and without its ranks. By the end of Reagan's second term, retrospective studies of aspects of his administration, reflecting greater distance from events and more information than was available in their midst, began to appear. The body of works appraising Reagan administration ideas and actions in foreign relations is growing rapidly; this can be expected to continue for some time. Any bibliographic survey at this time clearly will soon be outdated. Nevertheless, it is useful to consider what has appeared thus far in relatively durable and therefore continually influential book form.

Several works have focused on Ronald Reagan himself. Among the more insightful are Lou Cannon, *Reagan* (New York: Putnam, 1982), Robert Dallek, *Ronald Reagan: The Politics of Symbolism* (Cambridge: Harvard University Press, 1984), Michael Paul Rogin, *Ronald Reagan, The Movie, and Other Episodes in Political Demonology* (Berkeley: University of California Press, 1987), and Mary E. Stuckey, *Getting into the Game: The Pre-Presidential Rhetoric of Ronald Reagan* (New York: Praeger, 1987). Thus far the most noteworthy attempt to come to terms with Reagan's background and the sources of his ideas has been Garry Wills, *Reagan's America: Innocents at Home* (New York: Doubleday, 1987).

The elections of 1980 and 1984, uncertain but influential expressions of public opinion and the source of Reagan's authority in foreign affairs as in other matters, have received considerable scrutiny. The campaigns are well described in Elizabeth Drew, *Portrait of an Election: The 1980 Presidential Campaign* (New York: Simon and Schuster, 1981) and *Campaign Journal: The Political Events of 1983–1984* (New York: Macmillan, 1985), and two books by Jack W. Germond and Jules Witcover, *Blue Smoke and Mirrors: How Reagan Won and Why Carter Lost the Election of 1980* (New York: Viking, 1981) and *Wake Us When It's Over: Presidential Politics of 1984* (New York: Macmillan, 1985). More analytical treatments of the two elections can be found in Thomas Ferguson and Joel Rogers, eds., *The Hidden Election: Politics and Economics in the 1980 Presidential Campaign* (New York: Pantheon, 1981) and Austin Ranney, ed., *The American Elections of 1980* (Washington, D.C.: American Enterprise Institute, 1981) and *The American Elections of 1984* (Durham, N.C.: Duke University Press, 1985).

Early studies of the Reagan administration include Lawrence I. Barrett, *Gambling with History: Reagan in the White House* (New York: Doubleday, 1983); Ronnie Dugger, *On Reagan: The Man and His Presidency* (New York: McGraw-Hill, 1983); and Mark Green and Gail MacColl, *There He Goes Again: Ronald Reagan's Reign of Error* (New York: Pantheon, 1983). Sidney Blumenthal, *Our Long National Daydream: A Political Pageant of the Reagan Era* (New York: Harper and Row, 1988) focused on the middle years of the administration, whereas Jane Mayer and Doyle McManus looked closely and quite critically at Reagan's second term in *Landslide: The Unmaking of the President, 1984–1988* (Boston: Houghton Mifflin, 1988). As the administration came to an end, attempts to sum it up included David Boaz, ed., *Assessing the Reagan Years* (Washington, D.C.: Cato Institute, 1988), Sidney Blumenthal and Thomas Byrne Edsall, eds., *The Reagan Legacy* (New York: Pantheon, 1988), and Bob Schieffer and Gary Paul Gates, *The Acting President* (New York: Dutton, 1988). Although more broadly conceived, all of these books contain considerable discussion of foreign relations.

Ronald Reagan's extraordinary success in conveying an appealing image and message to the American public stirred comment from many of the authors already cited and was the subject of two studies: Robert E. Denton, Jr., *The Primetime Presidency of Ronald Reagan: The Era of the Television Presidency* (New York: Praeger, 1988), and Mark Hertsgaard, *On Bended Knee: The Press and the Reagan Presidency* (New York: Farrar Straus Giroux, 1988).

A number of high administration officials published memoirs soon after leaving office and well before the end of the Reagan presidency. The rush to tell one's side of the story in various policy or personality disputes, especially if one lost out and left the government, quickly provided a substantial amount of information on the inner workings of the Reagan White House. The first of these "kiss and tell" memoirs to appear was by former Secretary of State Alexander M. Haig, Jr., *Caveat: Realism, Reagan, and Foreign Policy* (New York: Macmillan, 1984). Then came ex-budget director David A. Stockman, *The Triumph of Politics: How the Reagan Revolution Failed* (New York: Harper and Row, 1986) followed by Michael K. Deaver, *Behind the Scenes* (New York: William Morrow, 1987). As Reagan's presidency drew to a close, the pace of memoir publication increased. Especially (if not always intentionally) revealing on the process of foreign policy formulation and articulation were Donald T. Regan, *For the Record: From Wall Street to Washington* (San Diego: Harcourt Brace Jovanovich, 1988) and Larry Speakes, *Speaking Out: The Reagan Presidency from Inside the White House* (New York: Scribners, 1988). Further from the center of decision making and therefore providing other perspectives were Martin Anderson, *Revolution* (San Diego: Harcourt Brace Jovanovich, 1988) and Terrel H. Bell, *The Thirteenth Man: A Reagan Cabinet Memoir* (New York: Free Press, 1988).

Overviews of the foreign relations of the Reagan administration were provided early on by Kenneth A. Oye, Robert J. Lieber, and Donald Rothchild, eds., *Eagle Defiant: United States Foreign Policy in the 1980s* (Boston: Little Brown, 1983) and Jonathan Kwitny, *Endless Enemies: The Making of an Unfriendly World* (New York: Congdon and Weed, 1984). Later and more comprehensive views can be found in Morris H. Morley, ed, *Crisis and Confrontation: Ronald Reagan's Foreign Policy* (Totowa, N.J.: Rowen Littlefield, 1988); and a second volume edited by Oye, Lieber, and Rothchild, *Eagle Resurgent? The Reagan Era in American Foreign Policy* (Boston: Little Brown, 1987).

On the transcendent issue of U.S.-Soviet relations, a good starting point is Strobe Talbott, *The Russians and Reagan* (New York: Vintage, 1984). Later developments are treated in Seweryn Bialer and Michael Mandelbaum, eds., *Gorbachev's Russia and American Foreign Policy* (Boulder, Col.: Westview Press, 1988). A short-lived but significant crisis in U.S.-Soviet relations is best dealt with in Seymour M. Hersh, *"The Target Is Destroyed:" What Really Happened to Flight 007 and What America Knew About It* (New York: Random House, 1986).

The on-going question of nuclear disarmament is the concern of Robert Scheer in *With Enough Shovels: Reagan, Bush, and Nuclear War* (New York: Random House, 1982), as well as Strobe Talbott, *Deadly*

Gambits: The Reagan Administration and the Stalemate in Nuclear Arms Control (New York: Knopf, 1984) and *The Master of the Game: Paul Nitze and the Nuclear Peace* (New York: Knopf, 1988). Europe's important role in U.S.-Soviet relations is explored in Antony J. Blinken, *Ally versus Ally: America, Europe and the Siberian Pipeline Crisis* (New York: Praeger, 1987), Diana Johnstone, *The Politics of Euromissiles: Europe's Role in America's World* (London: Verso, 1984), and Joel Krieger, *Reagan, Thatcher, and the Politics of Decline* (New York: Oxford University Press, 1986).

Much of the published work on Reagan administration foreign relations focuses, appropriately, on Latin America. Excellent overviews can be found in Abraham F. Lowenthal, *Partners in Conflict: The United States and Latin America* (Baltimore: Johns Hopkins University Press, 1987), Lars Schoultz, *National Security and United States Policy Toward Latin America* (Princeton, N.J.: Princeton University Press, 1987), and Kevin J. Middlebrook and Carlos Rico, eds., *The United States and Latin America in the 1980s: Contending Perspectives on a Decade of Crisis* (Pittsburgh: University of Pittsburgh Press, 1986).

U.S. involvement in Central American affairs during the 1980s is well treated in Raymond Bonner, *Weakness and Deceit: U.S. Policy and El Salvador* (New York: Times Books, 1984), Peter Kornbluh, *Nicaragua, The Price of Intervention: Reagan's Wars Against the Sandinistas* (Washington, D.C.: Institute for Policy Studies, 1987), and Thomas W. Walker, ed., *Reagan versus the Sandinistas: The Undeclared War on Nicaragua* (Boulder, Col.: Westview Press, 1987), Robert A. Pastor, *Condemned to Repetition: The United States and Nicaragua* (Princeton, N.J.: Princeton University Press, 1987), and Roy Gutman, *Banana Diplomacy: The Making of American Policy in Nicaragua, 1981–1987* (New York: Simon and Schuster, 1988).

The 1983 U.S. invasion of the tiny Caribbean island nation of Grenada is examined in Hugh O'Shaughnessy, *Grenada: An Eyewitness Account of the U.S. Invasion and the Caribbean History that Provoked It* (New York: Dodd, Mead, 1984), Peter M. Dunn and Bruce W. Watson, eds., *American Intervention in Grenada: The Implications of Operation Urgent Fury* (Boulder, Col.: Westview Press, 1985), Scott Davidson, *Grenada: A Study in Politics and the Limits of International Law* (Brookfield, Vt.: Gover, 1987), and Reynold A. Burrowes, *Revolution and Rescue in Grenada: An Account of the U.S.-Caribbean Invasion* (Westport, Conn.: Greenwood, 1988).

The intelligence-gathering and covert operations of the Reagan administration reveal a great deal about the beliefs and tactics of those responsible for U.S. foreign relations in the 1980s. An excellent starting point for examining this topic is Rhodri Jeffreys-Jones, *The CIA and American Democracy* (New Haven: Yale University Press, 1989). Also of value are Bob Woodward, *Veil: The Secret War of the CIA, 1981– 1987* (New York: Simon and Schuster, 1987), David C. Martin and John Walcott, *Best Laid Plans: The Inside Story of America's War Against Terrorism* (New York: Harper and Row, 1988), Jonathan Kwitny, *The Crimes of Patriots: A True Tale of Dope, Dirty Money, and the CIA* (New York: Norton, 1987), and Steven Emerson, *Secret Warriors: Inside the Covert Military Operations of the Reagan Era* (New York: Putnam, 1988).

Apparently the largest and certainly the most controversial covert undertaking of the Reagan administration is dealt with effectively in Meyer and McManus, *Landslide,* already cited, as well as in Jonathan Marshall, Peter D. Scott, and Jane Hunter, *The Iran-Contra Connection: Secret Teams and Covert Operations in the Reagan Era* (Boston: South End Press, 1987), and Ben Bradlee, Jr., *Guts and Glory: The Rise and Fall of Oliver North* (New York: D. I. Fine, 1988). Two U.S. senators from Maine, Republican William S. Cohen and Democrat George J. Mitchell, convey a sense of public disenchantment with Reagan foreign policy as well as shed light on that policy in *Men of Zeal: A Candid Inside Story of the Iran-Contra Hearings* (New York: Viking, 1988). There will no doubt be much more on this as well as other aspects of Reagan foreign relations in memoirs and historical assessments yet to come.

Index

List of Contributors

JOHN LEWIS GADDIS is Distinguished Professor of History at Ohio University in Athens, Ohio. He is the author of, among other works, *Strategies of Containment: A Critical Appraisal of Postwar American National Security Policy* (1982) and *The Long Peace: Inquiries into the History of the Cold War* (1988).

AKIRA IRIYE was, at the time of the Akron symposium, Stein-Freiler Distinguished Service Professor of History at the University of Chicago. He has since become Professor of History at Harvard University. A past president of the American Historical Association, his many works on American-East Asian relations include *Power and Culture: The Japanese-American War, 1941–1945* (1981).

SUSANNE JONAS is a member of the research staff of Global Options in San Francisco and lectures at the University of California, Santa Cruz. Among her many publications on contemporary Latin America are *Revolution and Intervention in Central America* (1983), *Nicaragua Under Siege* (1984), and a forthcoming book on Guatemala.

PHILIP S. KHOURY is Associate Professor of History and Associate Dean of Humanities and Social Sciences at the Massachusetts Institute of Technology. He is the author of *Urban No-*

tables and Arab Nationalism: The Politics of Damascus, 1860–1920 (1983) and *Syria and the French Mandates: The Politics of Arab Nationalism* (1987), and coeditor of the forthcoming *Tribes and State Formation in the Middle East.*

DAVID E. KYVIG is Professor of History at the University of Akron in Ohio. A 1987–1988 Fulbright Professor at the University of Tromsø, Norway, he organized the "Reagan and the World" symposium.

GEIR LUNDESTAD was, at the time of the Akron symposium, Professor of History at the University of Tromsø in Norway and a fellow at the Woodrow Wilson Center for Scholars of the Smithsonian Institution in Washington, D.C. He has since become director of the Nobel Institute in Oslo, Norway, He is the author of *America, Scandinavia, and the Cold War* (1980) and *East, West, North, South* (1985, 1987).

ROBERT I. ROTBERG is Vice President for Academic Affairs at Tufts University in Medford, Massachusetts, and coeditor of the *Journal of Interdisciplinary History.* He is the author of *The Founder: Cecil Rhodes and the Pursuit of Power* (1988).